Pelican Books
The Child, the Family, and the Outside World

D. W. Winnicott was born in 1896 at Plymouth, Devon. He spent his childhood in Plymouth, where his father was a merchant. Later he went to the Leys School in Cambridge and then to Jesus College, Cambridge. He continued his studies as a medical student at St Bartholomew's Hospital in London. He was drawn towards clinical medicine and especially towards what is now called paediatrics, and apart from his year as Resident at St Bartholomew's his hospital appointments have all been at children's hospitals. At the Paddington Green Children's Hospital he was Physician with his own department, and retired after 40 years. During the last half of this period his department gradually changed into one which was involved particularly with child psychiatry rather than physical paediatrics, the change being due to the fact that he himself had in the meantime taken the psycho-analytic training. He eventually became President of the British Psycho-Analytical Society. He has always been interested in the presentation of ideas derived from paediatrics, child psychiatry, and psycho-analysis in language suitable for parents, teachers, social workers, etc. Apart from this he has contributed a series of scientific papers written specifically for psycho-analysts, and these have been collected together in book form. As part of his teaching activities Dr Winnicott has been continuously employed teaching psycho-analysts, child psychiatrists, teachers and social workers. He is now practising in psycho-analysis and child psychiatry.

D. W. Winnicott

The Child, the Family, and the Outside World

Penguin Books

Penguin Books Ltd, Harmondsworth,
Middlesex, England
Penguin Books Australia Ltd,
Ringwood, Victoria, Australia

First published 1964
Reprinted 1965, 1967, 1968, 1969, 1970
Copyright © D. W. Winnicott, 1957 and 1964

A large part of the material in this book was originally
published in two volumes – *The Child and the Family* and
The Child and the Outside World (1957) – by Tavistock
Publications Limited

Made and printed in Great Britain by Richard Clay
(The Chaucer Press) Ltd, Bungay, Suffolk
Set in Monotype Garamond

Contents

Introduction 9

Part Three: The Outside World

Much of this book is based on talks broadcast by the B.B.C. at various times, and I wish to express my gratitude to the producer, Miss Iza Benzie. I would like also to thank Dr Janet Hardenberg who helped to prepare the talks for a reading (as opposed to listening) audience when they were first published.

D. W. W.

Introduction

This book seems to me to need an introduction. It is about mothers and babies, and about parents and children, and towards the end it is about children at school and in the wider world. The language I have used grows up, so to speak, with the growing child, and I hope it alters to match the change from the intimacy of infant care to a more detached relationship that is appropriate when the child is older.

Although the early chapters are addressed intimately to mothers, I am certainly not putting forward the view that it is essential for the young mother to read books about child care. This would imply that she is more self-conscious about her state than she is. She needs protection and information, and she needs the best that medical science can offer in the way of bodily care. She needs a doctor and a nurse whom she knows, and in whom she has confidence. She also needs the devotion of a husband, and satisfying sexual experiences. But she does not necessarily need to be told in advance what being a mother feels like.

One of my main ideas is this, that the best mothering comes out of natural self-reliance and there is a distinction to be made between the things that may come naturally and the things that have to be learnt, and I try to distinguish between these so that what comes naturally may not be spoiled.

I believe there is a place for addressing mothers and fathers directly, because people want to know what is happening in the early stage of infancy, and somehow the subject comes more to life in this way than if I were to write about mothers and babies in the abstract.

People want to know about the beginnings of their lives, and I think they ought to want to know. It could be said that there is something missing in human society if children grow up and become in their turn fathers and mothers, but do not know and acknowledge just what their mothers did for them at the start.

By this I don't mean that children should thank their parents for conceiving them, or even for their cooperation in home-building and the management of family affairs. I am concerned with the mother's relation to her baby just before the birth and in the first weeks and months after the birth. I am trying to draw attention to the immense contribution to the individual and to society which the ordinary good mother with her husband in support makes at the beginning, and which she does *simply through being devoted to her infant*.

Is not this contribution of the devoted mother unrecognized precisely because it is immense? If this contribution is accepted it follows that everyone who is sane, everyone who feels himself to be a person in the world, and for whom the world means something, every happy person, is in infinite debt to a woman. At a time in earliest infancy when there was no perception of dependence, we were absolutely dependent.

Once again let me emphasize, the result of such recognition of the maternal role when it comes will not be gratitude or even praise. The result will be a lessening in ourselves of a fear. If our society delays making full acknowledgement of this dependence which is a historical fact in the initial stage of development of every individual, there must remain a block to ease and complete health, a block that comes from a fear. If there is no true recognition of the mother's part, then there must remain a vague fear of dependence. This fear will sometimes take the form of a fear of woman in general or fear of a particular woman, and at other times will take on less easily recognized forms, always including the fear of domination.

Unfortunately the fear of domination does not lead groups of people to avoid being dominated; on the contrary it draws them towards a specific or chosen domination. Indeed, were the psychology of the dictator studied one would expect to find that, among other things, in his own personal struggle he is trying to control the woman whose domination he unconsciously still fears, trying to control her by accommodating her, acting for her, and in turn demanding total subjection and 'love'.

Many students of social history have thought that fear of

woman is a powerful cause of the seemingly illogical behaviour of human beings in groups, but it is seldom traced to its root. Traced to its root in the history of each individual, this fear of woman turns out to be a fear of recognizing the fact of dependence, the initial dependence of earliest infancy. There are therefore good social reasons for instigating research into the very early stages of the infant–mother relationship.

At present the importance of the mother at the start is often denied, and instead it is said that in the early months it is only a technique of bodily care that is needed, and that therefore a good nurse will do just as well. We even find mothers (not, I hope, in this country) being told that they *must mother* their infants, this being the most extreme degree of denial that 'mothering' grows naturally out of being a mother.

Administrative tidiness, the dictates of hygiene, a laudable urge towards the promotion of bodily health, these and all sorts of other things get between the mother and her baby, and it is unlikely that the mothers themselves will rise up in concerted effort to protest against interference. I write this book because someone must act for the young mothers who are having their first and second babies, and who are necessarily themselves in a dependent state. I hope to give them support in their reliance on their natural tendencies, while at the same time paying full tribute to the skill and care of those who give help where the mother and father and the various parent-substitutes need help.

Part One

Mother and Child

Chapter 1

A Man Looks at Motherhood

To begin with, you will be relieved to know that I am not going to be telling you what to do. I am a man, and so I can never really know what it is like to see wrapped up over there in the cot a bit of my own self, a bit of me living an independent life, yet at the same time dependent and gradually becoming a person. Only a woman can experience this, and perhaps only a woman can imaginatively experience it, as she has to do when by bad luck of one kind or another the actual experience is lacking.

What is there for me to do, then, if I am not going to give instructions? I'm used to having mothers bring their children to me, and when this happens we see what we want to talk about right before our eyes. The baby is jumping about on the mother's knee, reaching out for things on my desk, climbing down on to the floor and crawling round; clambering up on the chairs, or pulling books out of the book-cases; or perhaps clinging to mother in dread of the white-coated doctor who will surely be a monster who eats children if they are nice, and who does worse things if they are nasty. Or an older child is at a separate table drawing pictures while mother and I are trying to piece together the history of his development, and trying to see where things started to go wrong. The child is listening out of one ear to make sure we are up to no mischief, and at the same time is communicating with me without speaking, by the drawings which I go over to see from time to time.

How easy is all this, and how different is my task now, when I have to build baby and small child out of my imagination and experience!

You have had the same difficulty. If I cannot communicate with you, what did you feel like having a baby a few weeks old, not knowing what was or was not there to communicate with? If you are thinking this out, try to remember at what age your baby or babies seemed to notice you as a person, and what made you feel fairly sure at that exciting moment that you were two people communicating with each other. You did not have to do everything from different sides of the room, by talking. What language would you have used? No, you found yourself concerned with management of the baby's body, and you liked it to be so. You knew just how to pick the baby up, how to put the baby down, and how to leave well alone, letting the cot act for you; and you had learnt how to arrange the clothes for comfort and for preserving the baby's natural warmth. Indeed, you knew all this when you were a little girl and played with dolls. And then there were special times when you did definite things, feeding, bathing, changing napkins, and cuddling. Sometimes the urine trickled down your apron or went right through and soaked you as if you yourself had let slip, and you didn't mind. In fact by these things you could have known that you were a woman, and an ordinary devoted mother.

I am saying all this because I want you to know that this man, nicely detached from real life, free from the noise and smell and responsibility of child care, does know that the mother of a baby is tasting real things, and that she would not miss the experience for worlds. If we understand each other thus far, you will perhaps let me talk about being an ordinary devoted mother and managing the earliest stages of the life of a new human being. I cannot tell you exactly what to do, but I can talk about what it all means.

In the ordinary things you do you are quite naturally doing very important things, and the beauty of it is that you do not have to be clever, and you do not even have to think if you do not want to. You may have been hopeless at arithmetic at school, or perhaps all your friends got scholarships, but you didn't like the sight of a history book, and so failed and left school early; or perhaps you would have done well if you hadn't had measles just before the exam. Or you may be really clever. But all this does not matter, and it hasn't anything to do with whether you are a good mother or not. If a child can play with a doll, you can be an ordinary devoted mother, and I believe you are just this most of the time. Isn't it strange that such a tremendously important thing should depend so little on exceptional intelligence!

If human babies are to develop eventually into healthy, independent, and society-minded adult individuals, they absolutely depend on being given a good start, and this good start is assured in nature by the existence of the bond between the baby's mother and the baby, the thing called love. So if you love your baby he or she is getting a good start.

Let me quickly say that I am not talking about sentimentality. You all know the kind of person who goes about saying, 'I simply *adore* babies'. But you wonder, do they love them? A mother's love is a pretty crude affair. There's possessiveness in it, appetite, even a 'drat the kid' element; there's generosity in it, and power, as well as humility. But sentimentality is outside it altogether, and is repugnant to mothers.

Now, it may be that you are an ordinary devoted mother, and you like being one without thinking about it. Artists are often the very people who hate thinking about art, and about the purpose of art. You, as a mother, may prefer to avoid thinking things out, so I want to warn you that in this book we are going to talk about the things a devoted mother does by just being herself. But a few will like to consider what they are doing. Probably some of you have finished with actual mothering, and your children have grown up and gone to school; you may then like to look back on the good things you did, and think about the way in which you laid the foundation for your children's development. If you did it all intuitively, probably that was the best way.

It is vitally important that we should get to understand the part played by those who care for the infant, so that we can protect the young mother from whatever tends to get between herself and her child. If she is without understanding of the thing she does so well she is without means to defend her position, and only too easily she spoils her job by trying to do what she is told, or what her own mother did, or what the books say.

Fathers come into this, not only by the fact that they can be good mothers for limited periods of time, but also because they can help to protect the mother and baby from whatever tends to interfere with the bond between them, which is the essence and very nature of child care.

In the following pages I shall be deliberately trying to put into words what a mother does when she is ordinarily and quite simply devoted to her baby.

We still have much to learn about infants at the beginning, and perhaps only mothers can tell us what we want to know.

Chapter 2

Getting to Know Your Baby

A woman's life changes in many ways when she conceives a child. Up to this point she may have been a person of wide interests, perhaps in business, or a keen politician, or an enthusiastic tennis player, or one who has always been ready for a dance or a 'do'. She may have tended to despise the relatively restricted lives of friends who have had a child, making rude remarks about their resemblance to vegetables. She may have been actually repelled by such technical details as the washing and airing of napkins. If she has been interested in children, her interest can be said to have been sentimental rather than practical. But sooner or later she herself becomes pregnant.

At first it may easily happen that she resents this fact, because she can see only too clearly what a terrible interference with her 'own' life it must mean. What she sees is true enough, and it would be silly for anyone to deny it. Babies are a lot of trouble, and they are a positive nuisance unless they are wanted. If a young woman has not yet begun to want the baby she is carrying she cannot avoid feeling that she is just unlucky.

Experience shows, however, that a change gradually takes place in the feelings as well as in the body of the girl who has conceived. Shall I say her interest gradually narrows down? Perhaps it is better to say that the direction of her interest turns from outwards to inwards. She slowly but surely comes to believe that the centre of the world is in her own body.

Perhaps some reader has just arrived at this stage, and is beginning to feel a little proud of herself, to feel she is someone who deserves respect, and for whom people should naturally make way on the pavement.

As you become more and more sure that you will soon become a mother you begin to put all your eggs into one basket, as the saying is. You begin to take the risk of allowing your-self to be concerned with one object, the little boy or girl human being that will be born. This little boy or girl will be yours in the deepest possible sense, and you will be his or hers.

To become a mother you go through a great deal, and I think that it is because you go through so much that you be-come able to see with especial clearness certain fundamental principles of infant care, so that it takes years of study for those who are not mothers to get as far in understanding as you may get in the ordinary course of your experience. But you may very well need support from those of us who study you, because superstitions and old wives' tales – some of them quite modern ones – come along and make you doubt your own true feelings.

Let us consider just what it is that the ordinary healthy-minded mother knows about her baby that is so vitally im-portant, and yet which is apt to be forgotten by those who only look on. I think the most important thing is that you easily feel that your baby is worth getting to know as a person, and worth getting to know from the earliest possible moment. No one who comes along to give you advice will ever know this as well as you know it yourself.

Even in the womb your baby is a human being, unlike any other human being, and by the time he is born he will have had quite a lot of experience, unpleasant as well as pleasant. It is, of course, easy to read into the face of a new-born baby things that are not there; though to be sure, a baby may look very wise at times, even philosophical. But if I were you I should not wait until the psychologists have decided how human a baby is at birth – I should just go right ahead and get to know this little person, and let him or her get to know you.

You already know something of your baby's characteristics because of the movements you have learned to expect from him inside your womb. If there has been a lot of movement you have wondered how much there is in the amusing saying that boys kick more than girls do; and in any case you have been pleased to have the actual sign of life and liveliness that this quickening has provided. And during this time the baby has, I suppose, come to know quite a lot about you. He has shared your meals. His blood has flowed more quickly when you drank a nice cup of tea in the morning, or when you ran to catch a bus. To some extent he must have known whenever you were anxious or excited or angry. If you have been restless he has become used to movement, and he may expect to be jogged on your knee or rocked in his cradle. If, on the other hand, you are a restful sort of person he has known peace, and may expect a quiet lap, and a still pram. In a way I should say that he knows you better than you know him, until he is born, and until you hear his cry, and are well enough to look at him, and to take him in your arms.

Babies and mothers vary tremendously in their condition after the event of birth, and perhaps it will be two or three days in your case before you and your baby are both fit to enjoy each other's company. But there is no real reason why you shouldn't start to get to know each other right away, if you are well enough. I know a young mother who made a very early contact with her baby boy, her first child. From the day of his birth, after each feed, he was put in a cradle and left by his mother's bed by the sensible matron of the nursing home. For a while he would lie awake in the quiet of the room, and the mother would put down her hand to him; and before he was a week old he began to catch hold of her fingers and look up in her direction. This intimate relationship continued without interruption and developed, and I believe it has helped to lay the foundation for the child's personality and for what we call his emotional development, and his capacity to withstand the frustrations and shocks that sooner or later came his way.

The most impressive part of your early contact with your baby will be at his feed-times, that is to say, when he is excited. You may be excited too, and you may be having feelings in your breasts which indicate that you are usefully excited, and that you are preparing to give milk. The baby is fortunate if he can take you and your excitements for granted at first, so that he can get on with the business of meeting and managing his own impulses and urges. For, according to my view, it is a most alarming thing to be an infant discovering the feelings that turn up when excitement comes along. Have you ever looked at it in that way?

You will see from this that you have to get to know your

infant in two states, when he is contented, and more or less unexcited, and when he is excited. At first, when he is unexcited, he will spend a great deal of his time asleep, but not all his time, and the moments of waking but peaceful life are precious. I know that some babies hardly ever manage to get satisfied and for a long time cry and show distress, even after feeding, and do not sleep easily, and in this case it is very difficult for the mother to make satisfactory contact. But in time things will probably settle down, and there will be some contentment, and perhaps during the bath-time there will be a chance for the beginnings of a human relationship.

One reason why you should get to know your baby both in contentment and in excitement is that he needs your help. And you cannot give this help unless you know where you are with him. He needs you to help him to manage the awful transitions from sleeping or waking contentment to all-out greedy attack. This could be said to be your first task as a mother, apart from routine, and a lot of skill is required which only the child's mother can possess, unless it be some good woman who adopts a baby in the first days after birth.

For instance, babies are not born with an alarm clock hanging round their necks, with instructions: feed three-hourly. Regular feeding is a convenience to the mother or to the nurse, and from the baby's point of view it may well turn out that regular feeding is the next best thing to having a pull whenever the impulse to feed turns up. But a baby does not necessarily start off *wanting* regular feeds; in fact, I think that what an infant expects to find is a breast that comes as it is wanted and disappears as it is unwanted. Occasionally a mother may have to give her breast in a gipsy way for a short period of time before she can adopt a rigid routine that suits her convenience. At any rate, it is well that when you are getting to know your baby you should know what it is that he starts off expecting, even if you decide that he cannot have it. And, if you know the whole of your infant, you will find that it is only when he is excited that he has such an imperious nature. In between times he is only too glad to find mother behind the breast or bottle, and to find the room behind mother, and the world outside the room. Whereas there is a tremendous amount to learn about your baby during his feed-times, you will see that I am suggesting that there is even more to learn about him while he is in his bath, or lying in his cot, or when you are changing his napkins.

If you are being looked after by a nurse, I hope she will understand me and not feel I am interfering when I say that you are at a disadvantage if your baby is only handed to you at feed-times. You need nurse's help, and you are not yet strong enough to top and tail the baby yourself. But if you do not know your sleeping baby, or your baby as he lies awake wondering, you must get a very funny impression of him when he is handed to you just for you to feed him. At this time he is a bundle of discontent, a human being to be sure, but one who has raging lions and tigers inside him. And he is almost certainly scared by his own feelings. If no one has explained all this to you, you may become scared too.

If, on the other hand, you already know your infant by watching him as he lies by your side, and by allowing him to play in your arms, and at your breast, you will see his excitement in its proper proportions and recognize it as a form of love. You will also be in a position to understand what is happening when he turns his head away and refuses to drink, like the proverbial horse taken to the water, or when he goes to sleep in your arms instead of working at his feed, or when he becomes agitated so that he is no good at his job. He is just scared of his own feelings, and you can help him at this point as no one else can by your great patience, and by allowing play, by allowing him to mouth the nipple, perhaps to handle it; anything that the infant can let himself enjoy, till at last he gains the confidence to take the risk and suck. This is not easy for you, because you have yourself to think of too, your breasts being either over-full or else waiting till the baby sucks before beginning to fill. But if you know what is happening you will be able to tide over the difficult time, and enable your baby to establish a good relation to you when he feeds.

He is not so silly, either. When you think that excitement means an experience for him rather like what being put in a den of lions would be for us, no wonder he wants to make sure you are a reliable milk-giver before he lets himself go for you. If you fail him it must feel to him as if the wild beasts will gobble him up. Give him time and he will discover you, and you will both eventually come to value even his greedy love of your breasts.

I think that an important thing about a young mother's experience of *early* contact with her baby is the reassurance that it gives her that her child is normal (whatever that may mean). In your case, as I have said, you may be too exhausted to start making friends with your baby on the first day, but it is well you should know that it is entirely natural that a mother should want to get to know her baby right away after the birth. This is not only because she longs to know him (or her), it is also – and it is this which makes it an urgent matter – because she has had all sorts of ideas of giving birth to something awful, something certainly not so perfect as a baby. It is as if human beings find it very difficult to believe that they are good enough to create within themselves something that is quite good. I doubt whether any mother really and fully believes in her child at the beginning. Father comes into this too, for he suffers just as much as mother does from the doubt that he may not be able to create a healthy normal child. Getting to know your baby is therefore in the first place an urgent matter, because of the relief the good news brings to both parents.

After this you will want to get to know your baby because of your love and pride. And then you will study him (or her) in detail so as to be able to give him the help he needs, help that he can only get from the one who knows him best, that is to say, from you, his mother.

All of this means that the care of a new-born infant is a whole-time job, and that it can be done well by only one person.

Chapter 3

The Baby as a Going Concern

I have been writing generally about mothers and their own babies. I was not specially out to tell mothers what to do, because they can get advice over details quite easily from Welfare Centres. In fact advice over details comes to them almost too easily, sometimes causing a feeling of muddle. I have chosen instead to write for those mothers who are ordinarily good at looking after their own babies, intending to help them to know what babies are like, and to show them a little of what is going on. The idea is that the more they know, the more they will be able to afford to trust their own judgement. It is when a mother trusts her own judgement that she is at her best.

It is surely tremendously important for a mother to have the experience of doing what she feels like doing, which enables her to discover the fullness of the motherliness in herself; for just as a writer is surprised by the wealth of ideas that turn up when he puts his pen to paper, so the mother is constantly surprised by what she finds in the richness of her minute-to-minute contact with her own baby.

In fact, one might ask how can a mother learn about being a mother in any other way than by taking full responsibility? If she just does what she is told, she has to go on doing what she is told, and to improve she can only choose somebody better to tell her what to do. But if she is feeling free to act in the way that comes naturally to her, she grows in the job.

This is where the father can help. He can help provide a space in which the mother has elbow-room. Properly protected by her man, the mother is saved from having to turn outwards to deal with her surroundings at the time when she is wanting so much to turn inwards, when she is longing to be concerned with the inside of the circle which she can make with her arms, in the centre of which is the baby. This period of time in which the mother is naturally preoccupied with the one infant does not last long. The mother's bond with the baby is very powerful at the beginning, and we must do all we can to enable her to be preoccupied with her baby at this, the natural time.

Now it so happens that it is not only the mother that this experience is good for; the baby undoubtedly needs exactly this kind of thing too. We are only just beginning to realize how absolutely the new-born infant needs love of the mother. The health of the grown-up person is being founded throughout childhood, but the foundation of the health of the human being is laid by you in the baby's first weeks and months. Perhaps this thought can help a little when you feel strange at the temporary loss of your interest in world affairs. You are founding the health of a person who will be a member of our society. This is worth doing. The odd thing is that it is generally thought that the care of children is more difficult the greater the number being cared for. Actually I am sure that the fewer the children, the greater the emotional strain. Devotion to one child is the greatest strain of all, and it is a good job it only lasts for a while.

So here you are with all your eggs in one basket. What are you going to do about it? Well, enjoy yourself! Enjoy being thought important. Enjoy letting other people look after the world while you are producing a new one of its members. Enjoy being turned-in and almost in love with yourself, the baby is so nearly part of you. Enjoy the way in which your man feels responsible for the welfare of you and your baby. Enjoy finding out new things about yourself. Enjoy having more right than you have ever had before to do just what you feel is good. Enjoy being annoyed with the baby when cries and yells prevent acceptance of the milk that you long to be generous with. Enjoy all sorts of womanly feelings that you cannot even start to explain to a man. Particularly, I know you will enjoy the signs that gradually appear that the baby is a person, and that you are recognized as a person by the baby.

Enjoy all this for your own sake, but the pleasure which you can get out of the messy business of infant care happens to be vitally important from the baby's point of view. The baby does not want to be given the correct feed at the correct time, so much as to be fed by someone who loves feeding her own baby. The baby takes for granted all things like the softness of the clothes and having the bath water at the right temperature. What cannot be taken for granted is the mother's pleasure that goes with the clothing and bathing of her own baby. If you are there enjoying it all, it is like the sun coming out, for the baby. The mother's pleasure has to be there or else the whole procedure is dead, useless, and mechanical.

This enjoyment, which comes naturally in the ordinary way, can of course be interfered with by your worries, and worry depends a great deal on ignorance. It is rather like the relaxation methods in childbirth, about which you may perhaps have read. The people who write these books do all they can to explain just what happens during pregnancy and childbirth, so that mothers can relax, which means stop worrying about the unknown, and, as it were, lie back on natural processes. So much of the pain of childbirth does not belong to childbirth itself but to the tightness that comes from fear, chiefly from fear of the unknown. That is all explained to you, and if you have a good doctor and nurse available you can bear the pain which cannot be avoided.

In the same way, after the child is born, the pleasure that you get looking after the baby depends on your not being tense and worried because of ignorance and fear.

In these pages I want to give mothers information, so that they will know more than they did about what is going on in the baby, and so that they will see how the baby needs just exactly what a mother does well if she is easy, natural, and lost in the job.

I shall talk about the baby's body and what goes on inside; and I shall talk about the baby's developing person, and I shall talk about the way you introduce the world in small doses, so that the baby is not confused.

Now I want to make just one thing clear. It is this. Your baby does not depend on you for growth and development. Each baby is a *going concern*. In each baby is a vital spark, and this urge towards life and growth and development is a part of the baby, something the child is born with and which is carried forward in a way that we do not have to understand. For instance, if you have just put a bulb in the window-box you know perfectly well that you do not have to make the bulb grow into a daffodil. You supply the right kind of earth or fibre and you keep the bulb watered just the right amount, and the rest comes naturally, because the bulb has life in it. Now, the care of infants is very much more complicated than the care of a daffodil bulb, but the illustration serves my purpose because, both with the bulb and with the infant, there is something going on which is not your responsibility. The baby was conceived in you and from that moment became a lodger in your body. After birth the baby became a lodger in your arms. This is a temporary affair. It will not last for ever, in fact it will not last for long. The baby will only too soon be at school. Just at the moment this lodger is tiny and weak in body, and needing the special care that comes from your love. This does not alter the fact that the tendency towards life and growth is something inherent in the baby.

I wonder whether you feel at all relieved to hear somebody say this? I have known mothers whose enjoyment of their motherhood was spoiled by the fact that they felt somehow responsible for the aliveness of the baby. If the baby slept they would go over to the cot rather hoping that he or she would wake and so show signs of liveliness. If the baby were sullen they would play about, and poke his face, trying to produce a smile, which of course meant nothing to the infant. It was just a reaction. Such people are always jogging babies up and down on their knees trying to produce a giggle, or anything that reassures them themselves by indicating that the life process in the infant continues.

Some children are never allowed even in earliest infancy just to lie back and float. They lose a great deal and may altogether miss the feeling that they themselves want to live. It seems to me that if I can convey to you that there really is this living process in the baby (which, as a matter of fact, it is quite difficult to extinguish) you may be better able to enjoy the care of your baby. Ultimately, life depends less on the will to live than on the fact of breathing.

Some of you have created works of art. You have done drawings and paintings, or you have moulded out of clay, or you have knitted jumpers or made dresses. When you did these things, what turned up was made by you. Babies are different. The baby grows, and you are the mother providing a suitable environment.

Some people seem to think of a child as clay in the hands of a potter. They start moulding the infant, and feeling responsible for the result. This is quite wrong. If this is what you feel, then you will be weighed down with responsibility which you need not take at all. If you can accept this idea of a baby as a going concern you are then free to get a lot of interest out of looking to see what happens in the development of the baby while you are enjoying responding to his or her needs.

Chapter 4

Infant Feeding

Since the beginning of this century a great deal of work has been done on infant feeding, and doctors and physiologists have written many books and innumerable scientific articles, each adding a bit to our knowledge. The result of all this work is that it is now possible to distinguish between two sets of things, those of a physical or biochemical or substantial kind, which no one could know about intuitively, or without deep learning in scientific matters, and those of a psychological kind, which people have been able to know always, both by feeling and by simple observation.

For instance, to go to the root of the matter right away, infant feeding is a matter of infant–mother relationship, a putting into practice of a love relationship between two human beings. It was difficult, however, for this to be accepted (although it was felt to be true by mothers) until many difficulties had been cleared away by study of the physical side of the problem. At any period of the world's history a natural mother leading a healthy life must easily have thought of infant feeding simply as a relationship between her baby and herself; but there was at the same time the mother whose baby died of diarrhoea and sickness; she did not know it was a germ that had killed her baby, and so she must have felt convinced that her milk was bad. Infant disease and death make mothers lose confidence in themselves, and make them look for authoritative advice. In countless ways physical disease has complicated the problem as seen by the mother. In fact, it is only because of the great advances in knowledge of physical health and physical disease that we can now return to the main thing which is the emotional situation, the feeling bond between mother and baby. It is this feeling bond that must be developing satisfactorily if feeding is to go well.

Nowadays the doctors of the body understand enough

about rickets to prevent its occurrence; they understand enough about the dangers of infection to prevent the blindness that used to follow gonococcal infection of the baby at birth; enough about the danger of tuberculous milk from infected cows to prevent much of the tuberculous meningitis that used to be common and fatal; enough about scurvy to have virtually eliminated it. And now it has suddenly become urgent for those of us who concern ourselves chiefly with feelings to state as accurately as we can the psychological problem which confronts every mother, however complete the absence of bodily disease and disorder due to the doctors' skill.

No doubt we cannot yet accurately state the psychological problem which confronts every mother of a new-born baby, but an attempt can be made, and mothers can take part in correcting what is wrong in what I say and adding what is left out.

I will take a chance on it. If the mother we are thinking about is ordinarily healthy, living in an ordinarily tolerable home kept by her and her husband, and if we pretend that the baby arrived in a healthy state and at the right time, then there is something remarkably simple to be said: in these circumstances, infant feeding is just a part, one of the more important parts it is true, of a relationship of two human beings. These two, mother and new-born baby, are ready to be bound to each other by tremendously powerful bonds of love, and they naturally have to get to know each other before taking the great emotional risks involved. Once they have come to a mutual understanding – which they may do at once, or which they may do only after a struggle – they rely on each other and understand each other, and the feeding begins to look after itself.

In other words, if the relationship between mother and baby has started, and is developing naturally, then there is no need for feeding techniques, and weighings and all sorts of investigations; the two together know what is just right better than any outsider ever can. In such circumstances an infant will take the right amount of milk at the right speed, and will know when to stop. And in that case even the baby's digestion and excretions do not have to be watched by outsiders. The whole physical process works just because the emotional relationship is developing naturally. I would even go further and say that a mother in such circumstances can learn about babies from her baby, just as the baby learns about the mother from her.

The real trouble is that so great feelings of pleasure belong to the intimate bodily and spiritual bond that can exist between a mother and her baby that mothers easily fall a prey to the advice of people who seem to say that such feelings must not be indulged in. Surely the modern puritan is to be found in this realm of infant feeding! Fancy keeping a baby away from his mother after he is born till he has lost his one possibility (through his sense of smell) of feeling he has found her again after he had lost her! Fancy wrapping up the baby while he is feeding so that he cannot handle the breasts or the bottle, with the result that he can only take part in the proceedings by 'Yes' (sucking) or 'No' (turning the head away or sleeping)! Fancy starting off feeding a baby by the clock before he has gained the feeling that there really is anything outside himself and his desires at all.

In the natural state (by which I mean when the two human beings involved are healthy) techniques and quantities and timing can be left to nature. This means, in practice, that the mother can allow the infant to decide what it is in his power to decide, because she is easily able to decide and provide what it is her job to give in the way of management, as well as in the form of actual milk.

It may be thought imprudent of me to say these things because so few mothers are free from personal difficulties, and from the tendency to worry that makes them need support; also, there undoubtedly are mothers who neglect their babies or are cruel to them. However, it is my opinion that even mothers who know they need advice all along the line are nevertheless helped by having these basic facts in front of them. If such a mother is to learn to make a job of her second or third baby's early contact with her, she must know what she was aiming at even with her first baby over whom she needed so much help; she aims at being independent of advice in her actual management of her own babies.

I would say that natural feeding is given exactly when the baby wants it, and ceases as he ceases to want it. This is the basis. On this, and only on this, can an infant start to compromise with his mother, the first compromise being the acceptance of regular and reliable feeding, say three-hourly, which is convenient for mother, and which can yet feel to the infant like the fulfilment of his own desire, if only he can arrange to be hungry regularly at three-hourly intervals. If this interval is too long for the child in question, distress ensues, and the quickest method of restoring confidence is for the mother to feed as and when required for a new period, returning to a suitable regular timing as the baby becomes able to tolerate it.

Again, this may seem rather wild. A mother who has been schooled into training her infant to regular habits, starting with regular three-hourly feeds, feels actually wicked if told to feed her baby just like a gipsy. As I have said, she easily feels scared of the very great pleasure involved in this, and feels she will be blamed by her in-laws and the neighbours for whatever goes wrong from that day forward. The main trouble is that people easily feel overwhelmed by the responsibility of having a baby at all, and they only too readily welcome the rule and the regulation and the precept, which makes life less risky even if a trifle boring. To some extent, however, the medical and nursing professions are to blame, and we must quickly withdraw whatever we have put between the mother and her baby. Even the idea of natural feeding would be harmful if it were to become a thing to be consciously aimed at, because it was said to be good by the authorities.

As to the theory that training baby must start as early as possible, the truth is that training is out of place until the infant has accepted the world outside himself and come to terms with it. And the foundation of this acceptance of external reality is the first brief period in which a mother naturally follows the desires of her infant.

You see that I am not saying that we can walk out of the infant welfare centres and leave the mothers and babies to cope with all the problems of basic diet, vitamins, vaccinations, and the proper way to wash napkins. What I am saying is that doctors and nurses should be aiming at so managing this physical side that nothing can disturb the delicate mechanism of the developing infant–mother relationship.

Of course, if I were talking to nurses who look after babies who are not their own, I should have a lot to say about their difficulties and disappointments. In her book, *The Nursing Couple*,* my late friend Dr Merell Middlemore wrote:

It is not surprising that roughness in the nurse should sometimes arise from nervousness. She follows the fortunes and failures of the nursing couple from feed to feed and, up to a point, their interests are her own. She may find it hard to watch the mother's clumsy efforts to feed the child, and may at the last feel driven to interfere because she thinks she can put things right. Her own maternal instinct is, as it were, roused to compete with the mother's, instead of reinforcing it.

Mothers reading what I have written must not be too upset if they have failed in their first contact with one of their children. There are so many reasons why there must be failures, and much can be done at a later date to make up for what has gone wrong, or has been missed. But the risk of making some mothers unhappy must be taken if one is to try to give support to those mothers who can succeed, and who are succeeding, in this the most important of all mothers' tasks. At any rate, I must risk hurting some who are in difficulties if I am to try to convey my opinion that if a mother is managing her relation to her baby *on her own*, she is doing the best that she can do for her child, for herself, and for society in general.

In other words, the only true basis for a relation of a child to mother and father, to other children, and eventually to society, is the first successful relationship between the mother and baby, between two people, with not even a regular feeding-rule coming between them, nor even a rule that baby must be breast-fed. In human affairs, the more complex can only develop out of the more simple.

* *The Nursing Couple*, Merell P. Middlemore, M.D., Hamish Hamilton Medical Books.

Chapter 5

Where the Food Goes

When babies begin to feel hungry something is beginning to come alive in them which is ready to take possession of them. You yourself begin to make certain noises to do with the preparation of the feed which the baby knows as a sign that the time is coming when it will be safe to let eagerness for food ripen into a terrific urge. You can see saliva flowing out, because small babies don't swallow their saliva – they show the world by dribbling that they have an interest in things they can get hold of with their mouths. Well, this is only saying that the baby is getting excited, and particularly excited in the mouth. The hands also play their part in the search for satisfaction. So when you give the baby food, you are fitting in with a tremendous desire for food. The mouth is prepared. The pads on the lips are very sensitive at this time and they help to provide a high degree of pleasurable mouth sensation which the baby will never have again in later life.

A mother actively adapts to her baby's needs. She likes to. Because of her love she is expert at making delicate adjustments in her management which other people wouldn't think worth while, and wouldn't be able to know about. Whether you are feeding at the breast or the bottle, the baby's mouth becomes very active and milk goes from you or the bottle into the mouth.

There is generally thought to be a difference here between the breast- and bottle-fed baby. The breast-fed baby gets behind the root of the nipple and chews with the gums. This can be quite painful for the mother, but the pressure there pushes the milk that is in the nipple into the mouth. The milk is then swallowed. The bottle-fed baby, however, has to employ a different technique. In this case the accent is on the sucking, which can be a relatively minor matter in the breast experience.

Some babies on the bottle need a fairly large hole in the teat

...cy want to get the milk without sucking until they nave learned to suck. Others suck right away and get swamped if the hole is too big.

If you are using a bottle, you will have to be prepared to make changes in what you are doing in a more conscious way than you would be if you were feeding at the breast. The breast-feeding mother relaxes, she feels the blood going to her breasts, and the milk just comes. When she is bottle-feeding she has to keep her wits about her. She keeps on taking the bottle out of the baby's mouth and letting some air into it, because otherwise the vacuum in the bottle becomes so great that the baby can't get any milk out. She lets the milk cool to almost the right temperature, and tests it by putting the bottle against her arm; and she has a can of hot water by her to stand the bottle in, in case the baby is slow and the milk cools down too much.

Well, now we are concerned with what happens to the milk. We could say that the baby knows a lot about the milk up to the moment when it is swallowed. There it is going into the mouth, and giving a definite sensation to the mouth, and having a definite taste. This is undoubtedly very satisfactory. And then it is swallowed. This means it is almost lost from the baby's point of view. Fists and fingers are better in this respect, for they stay put, and remain available. Swallowed food is not completely lost, however, not while it is in the stomach. From this the food can still be returned. Babies seem to be able to know of the state of their stomachs.

You probably know that the stomach is a small organ shaped rather like a baby's bottle swung across from left to right under the ribs, and it is a muscle, rather a complicated one, with a wonderful capacity for doing just what mothers do to their babies; that is, it adapts to new conditions. It does this automatically unless disturbed by excitement, fear, or anxiety, just as mothers are naturally good mothers unless they are tense and anxious. It is rather like a miniature good mother inside. When a baby feels at ease (or what we call relaxed when we are talking about grown-up people) this muscular container, which we call the stomach, behaves itself well. That means that it keeps up a certain tension within itself and yet maintains its shape and its position.

So the milk is in the stomach, and is held there. And now starts a series of processes which we call digestion. There is always fluid in the stomach, digestive juices, and at the top end there is always air. This air has a special interest for mothers and babies. When the baby swallows the milk there is an increase in the amount of fluid in the stomach. If you and the baby are fairly calm the pressure in the stomach-wall adapts itself and loosens up a bit; the stomach gets bigger. The baby is usually a bit excited, however, and the stomach therefore takes a little while to adapt. The temporarily increased pressure in the stomach is uncomfortable, and a quick way out of the trouble is for the baby to belch a little wind. For this reason, after you have fed your baby, or even in the middle of a feed, you may find it a good idea to expect a little wind, and if the baby is upright when belching you are much more likely to get wind by itself, instead of a return of some of the milk along with it. That is why you can see mothers putting their babies up on their shoulders and just patting the back a little, because the patting stimulates the stomach muscle and makes the baby more liable to belch.

Of course it very often happens that the baby's stomach adapts so quickly to the feed, and accepts the milk so easily, that there is no need for any belching at all. But if the mother of the baby is in a tense state herself (as she may well be sometimes) then the baby gets into a tense state too, and in that case the stomach will take longer to adapt to the increase in the amount of food in it. If you understand what is going on, you will be able to manage this wind business quite easily, and you will not be puzzled when one feed is quite different from another, or when one baby is different from another baby in this matter of wind.

If you do not understand what is going on, you are bound to be flummoxed. A neighbour says to you, 'Be sure you get some wind up after the baby's feed!' Not knowing the facts you can't argue so you plant the baby on your shoulder and vigorously pat the back, trying to get up this wind which you feel *has* to be produced. It can become a kind of religion. In that way you are imposing your own (or your neighbour's) ideas on the baby, and interfering with the natural way, which is after all the only good kind of way.

Well, this little muscular container keeps the milk for a certain length of time, until the first stage in digestion has occurred. One of the first things that happens to the milk is that it becomes curdled. That is the first stage in the natural process of digestion. In fact in making a junket you imitate what happens in the stomach. Don't be alarmed, therefore, if your baby brings up some curdled milk. It ought to be so. Also babies are very easily a little bit sick.

In this period, in which things are going on in the stomach itself, it is a very good idea if the baby is able to be quiet. Whether you manage this best by putting the baby in a cot after the feed, or by gently carrying him round for a little while, I must leave to you, because no two mothers and no two babies are alike. In the easiest circumstances the baby just lies back and seems to be contemplating the inside. There can be a good feeling inside at this time, because the blood goes to the active part, and this gives a nice warm sensation in the baby's belly. Disturbances, distractions, and excitements during this early part of the digestive processes can easily cause discontented crying, or can lead either to vomiting, or else to a too early passing on of the food before it has really undergone all the changes which it should undergo in the stomach itself. I think you know how important it is to keep neighbours out when you are feeding your child. This does not apply simply to the time when you are giving the feed. The feeding time continues right on to the time when the food leaves the stomach, and it is rather like the important part of a solemn occasion which seems to be spoiled if an aeroplane passes overhead. This solemn period extends to include the period after feeding, when the food is not yet fully accepted.

If all goes well, there comes an end to the particular sensitive time, and you begin to hear gurglings and rumblings. This means that the part of the digestion of the milk which goes on in the stomach is becoming completed, and quite automatically the stomach now tends to squirt more and more of the partially digested milk through a valve into what we might call the guts.

Now, you do not have to know much about what happens in the guts. The continuation of the digestion of the milk is a very complex process, but gradually the digested milk starts to get absorbed into the blood and to be carried to every part of the body. It is interesting to know that soon after the milk leaves the stomach bile is added. This comes down from the liver at the appropriate moment, and it is because of bile that the contents of the guts have their particular colour. You may have had catarrhal jaundice yourself and so you know how horrid it feels when the bile cannot go from the liver into the guts, in that case because of inflammatory swelling in the little tube that carries it. The bile (in catarrhal jaundice) goes into your blood instead of into your guts, and makes you yellow all over. But when the bile goes the right way just at the right moment, from the liver to the guts, it makes the baby feel good.

Well, if you look it up in a physiology book you will be able to find out all that happens in the further digestion of the milk, but the details do not matter if you are a mother. The point is that the gurglings indicate that the period in which the child is sensitive is at an end, and the food is now really inside. From the infant's point of view this new stage must be a mystery, as physiology is beyond the infant mind. *We* know, however, that in various ways the food is absorbed from the guts, and it eventually gets distributed round the body and by means of the blood stream gets carried to every part of the tissues, which are all the time growing. In a baby these tissues are growing at a tremendous pace, and they need regularly repeated supplies.

Chapter 6

The End of the Digestive Process

In the last chapter I traced the fate of the milk as it was swallowed, digested, and absorbed. Here in the guts of the baby there is a great deal that goes on that does not concern the mother, and from the baby's point of view all this part of the process is a mystery. Gradually, however, the baby becomes involved again at the last stage, which we call excretion, and so the mother is involved too, and she can play her part best if she knows what is going on.

The fact is that the food is not all absorbed; even perfectly good breast milk leaves some kind of residue, and in any case there is the wear and tear of the guts. One way and another there is a lot left over, and it has to be got rid of.

The various things that go to make up what is going to be the motion gradually get passed on to the lower end of the guts towards the opening which is called the anus. How is this done? The stuff is moved on by a series of contraction waves which keep on going down the length of the guts. By the way, did you know that the food has to go through a narrow tube twenty feet long in a grown-up? In a baby the guts are about twelve feet long.

I sometimes have a mother say to me, 'The food went right through 'im, doctor.' It seemed to the mother that as soon as some food went into the baby it came out again at the other end. That is what it looks like, but it isn't true. The point is that the baby's guts are sensitive, and the taking of food starts up the waves of contraction in the guts; when these reach the lower end a motion is passed. Ordinarily the last part of the guts, the rectum, is more or less empty. These contraction waves get busy when there is much to be passed along, or if the baby is excited, or if the guts are inflamed by infection. Gradually, and only gradually, the infant gets some measure of control, and I want to tell you how this happens.

At first we can imagine that the rectum begins to fill simply because there is a large amount of residue waiting to pass down. Probably the actual stimulus for the bowel movement comes from the digestive process set up by the last feed. Sooner or later the rectum is filled. The infant has not known much about the stuff while it was higher up, but the filling of the rectum produces a definite sensation which is not un-pleasurable, and it makes the baby want to pass the motion right out. At first we need not expect the baby to hold it in the rectum. You know only too well that in the early stages of infant care the changing and washing of napkins looms large. If there must be clothes, then there has to be a frequent chang-ing of napkins, otherwise the motion left for a long time in contact with the skin causes soreness. This is especially true if for some reason or other the motion has been passed on quickly and is therefore liquid. This napkin business cannot be got rid of by hasty training. If you carry on with the good work, and play for time, then things begin to happen.

You see, if the motion is held by the baby at the last stage in the rectum, it gets dried; water is absorbed from it as it waits there. The motion is then passed on as a solid thing which the baby can enjoy passing; in fact, at the moment of passing the motion there can be such an excitement just there that the baby cries from excess of feeling. You see what you are doing by leaving the matter to your baby (although helping in so far as the baby cannot manage alone)? You are giving every possible chance for him to find from experience that it feels good to collect the stuff and hold it for a while before passing it on, and even for the baby to discover that the result is in-teresting, and that in fact defecation can be an extremely satisfactory experience if all goes well. The establishment of this healthy attitude of the baby towards these things is the only good foundation for anything you may want to do at a later date in the way of training.

Perhaps someone told you to hold your baby out regularly after feeds from the start, with the idea of getting in a bit of training at the earliest possible moment. If you do this you should know that what you are doing is trying to save your-self the bother of dirty napkins. And there is a lot to be said for this. But the baby is not anywhere near being able to be trained yet. If you never allow for his or her own development in these matters, you interfere with the beginnings of a natural process. Also you are missing good things. For instance, if you wait you will sooner or later discover that the baby, lying over there in the cot, finds a way of letting you know that a motion has been passed; and soon you will even get an inkling that there is going to be a motion. You are now at the beginning of a new relationship with the baby, who cannot communicate with you in an ordinary grown-up way, but who has found a way of talking without words. It is as if he said, 'I think I am going to want to pass a motion; are you interested?' and you (without exactly saying so) answer 'Yes,' and you let him know that if you are interested this is not because you are frightened that he will make a mess, and not because you feel you ought to be teaching him how to be clean. If you are interested it is because you love your baby in the way mothers do, so that whatever is important to the baby is also important to you. So you will not mind if you got there late, because the important thing was not keeping the baby clean, it was the answering of the call of a fellow human being.

Later on, your relationship to the infant in these terms will become richer; sometimes a baby will feel frightened of the motion that is coming, and sometimes he will feel that it is something valuable. Because what you do is based on the simple fact of your love you soon become able to distinguish between the times when you are helping your baby to be rid of bad things and the times when you are receiving gifts.

There is a practical point worth mentioning here. When a nice satisfactory motion has been passed you might think that that was the end of everything, and you pack the baby up again and get on with whatever you are doing. But the baby may show new discomfort, or may dirty the clean napkin almost immediately. It is extremely likely that a first emptying of the rectum will be followed almost immediately by a certain amount of refilling. If you are not in a hurry, and you can afford to wait, the baby will be able to pass this instalment too when the next waves of contraction come down. This might happen, and it might happen again. By not being in a hurry you leave your baby with an empty rectum. This keeps the rectum sensitive, and the next time it fills, some hours later, the baby will once more go over the whole procedure in a natural way. Mothers who are always in a hurry always have to leave their babies with something in the rectum. This will either be passed out, causing unnecessary dirtying of napkins, or else it will be held in the rectum which therefore becomes less sensitive, and the beginnings of the next experience will be interfered with to some extent. Unhurried management over a long period of time naturally lays the basis for a sense of order in the baby's relation to his excretory functions. If you are in a hurry, and cannot allow for the *total* experience, the baby will start off in a muddle. The baby who is not in a muddle will be able to follow you later on, and gradually give up some of the tremendous pleasure that belongs to the doing of a motion just exactly when the impulse comes. The baby does this not simply to comply with your wish that as few messes as possible be made, but out of a wish to wait for you, so as to get into touch with your liking to look after all that has to do with your own baby. Much later on the baby will be able to gain control down there, and to make messes when the idea is to dominate over you, and to hold things back till the convenient moment comes when the idea is to please you.

I could tell you about plenty of babies who never had a chance to find themselves in this important matter of the passing of motions. I know of a mother who practically never let any of her babies have a natural motion. She had a theory that the motion in the rectum poisons the baby in some way or other. This is simply not true, and babies and small children can hold their motions there for days without being really harmed. This mother was always interfering with each baby's rectum with soapsticks and enemas, and the result was more than chaotic. Certainly she had no hope whatever of producing happy children who could easily be fond of her.

The same general principles underly the other kind of excretion, the passing of urine.

Water is absorbed into the blood stream, and what is not needed is excreted by the baby's kidneys and passed to the bladder along with waste products dissolved in it. The baby does not know anything till the bladder begins to fill, and

43

then there develops an urge to pass the urine out. At first this is more or less automatic, but the baby gradually finds that there is a reward for holding back a little – after holding back the baby finds it pleasurable to get rid of the water. There develops another little orgy that enriches the life of the infant, that makes life worth living, and the body worth living in.

In the course of time this discovery of the infant, that waiting pays, can be used by you, because you can get to know by signs that something may be going to happen, and you can still further enrich the baby's experience by your interest in the procedure. In time the baby will like to wait, if not too long, just in order to get the whole thing within the love relationship that exists between the two of you.

You see how it is that the baby's mother is needed for the management of the excretions, just as she is needed for the feeding? Only the mother feels it is worth while to follow the infant's needs in detail, so enabling the exciting experience of the body to become part of a love relationship between two persons, the baby and herself.

When this is what happens, and when it is kept up over a period of time, what is called training can follow without much difficulty, because the mother has earned the right to make such demands as are not beyond the infant's capacity.

Here again is an example of the way in which the foundations of health are laid down by the ordinary mother in her ordinary loving care of her own baby.

Chapter 7

Close-up of Mother Feeding Baby

I have already said that the baby appreciates, perhaps from the very beginning, the *aliveness* of the mother. The pleasure the mother takes in what she does for the infant very quickly lets the infant know that there is a human being behind what is done. But what eventually makes the baby feel the person in the mother is perhaps the mother's special ability to put herself in the place of the infant, and so to know what the infant is feeling like. No book rules can take the place of this feeling a mother has for her infant's needs, which enables her to make at times an almost exact adaptation to those needs.

I will illustrate this by looking at the feeding situation, and by comparing two babies. One of them is fed by the mother at home, and the other is fed in an institution, a nice place, but a place where the nurses have a lot to do and there is no time for individual attention.

I will take the baby in the institution first. Hospital nurses who read this, and who do feed the babies in their care individually, must forgive me for using as an illustration the worst, and not the best, of what they can do.

Here then is the baby in the institution at feed-time, hardly knowing yet what to expect. The baby that we are considering does not know much about bottles or about people, but is beginning to be prepared to believe that something satisfactory may turn up. The baby is propped up a little in the cot, and a bottle with milk is so arranged with pillows that it reaches his mouth. The nurse puts the teat into the baby's mouth, waits for a few moments, and then goes off to look after some other baby who is crying. At first things may go fairly well, because the hungry baby is stimulated to suck from the teat and the milk comes, and it feels nice; but there the thing is, sticking in the mouth, and in a few moments it has become a sort of huge threat to existence. The baby cries or struggles, then the bottle drops out, and this produces relief, but only for a little while, because soon the baby begins to want to have another go, and the bottle does not come, and then crying restarts. After a while the nurse comes back and puts the bottle in the baby's mouth again, but by now the bottle, which looks the same as it did, from our point of view, seems to the baby like a bad thing. It has become dangerous. This goes on and on.

Now let us go over to the other extreme, to the baby whose own mother is available. When I see in what a delicate way a mother who is not anxious manages the same situation I am always astounded. You see her there, making the baby comfortable, and arranging a *setting* in which the feeding may happen, if all goes well. The setting is a part of a human relationship. If the mother is feeding by the breast we see how she lets the baby, even a tiny one, have the hands free so that as she exposes her breast the texture of the skin can be felt, and its warmth—moreover the distance of her breast from the baby can be measured, for the baby has only a little bit of the world in which to place objects, the bit that can be reached by mouth, hands, and eyes. The mother allows the baby's face to touch the breast. At the beginning babies do not know about breasts being part of mother. If the face touches the breast they do not know at the beginning whether the nice feeling comes in the breast or in the face. In fact babies play with their cheeks, and scratch them, just as if they were breasts, and there is plenty of reason why mothers allow for all the contact that a baby wants. No doubt a baby's sensations in these respects are very acute, and if they are acute we can be sure they are important.

The baby first of all needs all these rather *quiet* experiences which I am describing, and needs to feel held lovingly, that is, in an alive way, yet without fuss, and anxiety, and tenseness. This is the setting. Sooner or later there will be some kind of contact between the mother's nipple and the baby's mouth. It does not matter what exactly happens. The mother is there in the situation and part of it, and she particularly likes the intimacy of the relationship. She comes without preconceived notions as to how the baby ought to behave.

This contact of the nipple with the baby's mouth gives the

baby ideas! – 'perhaps there is something there outside the mouth worth going for'. Saliva begins to flow; in fact, so much saliva may flow that the baby may enjoy swallowing it, and for a time hardly needs milk. Gradually the mother enables the baby to build up in imagination the very thing that she has to offer, and the baby begins to mouth the nipple, and to get to the root of it with the gums and bite it, and perhaps to suck.

And then there is a pause. The gums let go of the nipple, and the baby turns away from the scene of action. The idea of the breast fades.

Do you see how important this last bit is? The baby had an idea, and the breast with the nipple came, and a contact was made. Then the baby was finished with the idea and turned away, and the nipple disappeared. This is one of the most important ways in which the experience of the baby we are now describing differs from that of the one that we placed in the busy institution. How does the mother deal with the baby's turning away? This baby does not have a thing pushed back into the mouth in order that sucking movements shall be started up again. The mother understands what the baby is feeling, because she is alive and has an imagination. She waits. In the course of a few minutes, or less, the baby turns once more towards where she is all the time willing to place the nipple, and so a new contact is made, just at the right moment. These conditions are repeated time and again, and the baby drinks not from a thing that contains milk, but from a personal possession lent for the moment to a person who knows what to do with it.

The fact that the mother is able to make such delicate adaptation shows that she is a human being, and the baby is not long in appreciating this fact.

I want to make rather a special thing out of the way the mother in our second illustration lets the baby turn away. It is especially here, where she takes the nipple away from the baby as the baby ceases to want it or to believe in it, that she establishes herself as the mother. This is such a delicate operation at the beginning that the mother cannot always succeed, and sometimes a baby will show a need to establish the right to the personal way by refusing food, turning the head away, or going to sleep. This is very disappointing for a mother who is longing to get on with being generous. Sometimes she cannot stand the tension in the breasts (unless someone has told her how to express milk so that she can afford to wait till the baby turns towards her). If mothers knew, however, that the turning away of the baby from the breast or from the bottle had a value, they might be able to manage these difficult phases. They would take the turning away, or the sleepiness, as an indication for special care. This means that everything must be done in the way of providing the right setting for the feed. The mother must be comfortable. The baby must be comfortable. Then there must be time to spare. And the baby's arms must be free. The baby must be able to have skin free with which to feel the skin of the mother. It may even be that a baby needs to be put naked on the mother's naked body. If there is difficulty, the one thing that is absolutely no use at all is the attempt to force the feeding. If there is a difficulty, it is only by giving the baby the setting to find the breast that there is any hope of establishing the right kind of feeding experience. Echoes of all this may appear at later stages in the infant's experiences.

While I am on this subject, I would like to talk about the position of the mother whose baby is just born. She has been through an anxious and severe experience, and she continues to need skilled help. She is still in the care of whoever has helped with the confinement. There are reasons why she is particularly liable just at this time to feel dependent, and to be sensitive to the opinions of any important woman who happens to be around, whether this be the matron of the hospital, or the midwife, or her own mother or mother-in-law. She is in a difficult position then. She has been preparing for this moment for nine months, and for reasons that I have tried to explain she is the best person to know what to do to get her baby to feed at the breast, and yet if the others who know so much are strong-minded, she can hardly be expected to fight them, certainly not until she has had two or three babies, and a lot of experience. The ideal thing, of course, is the happy relationship that often exists between maternity nurses or the midwife, and the mother.

If there is this happy relationship, the mother is given every chance to manage the first contact with the baby in her own way. The baby is beside her asleep most of the time, and she can keep on looking down into the cradle beside the bed to see whether it really is a nice human baby she has got. She gets used to her own baby's cry. If she is worried by the crying the baby is temporarily taken away while she sleeps, but is brought back. Then, when she senses that the baby begins to want food, or perhaps to want a general contact with her body, she is helped to take the baby into her arms and to nurse him. In the course of this sort of experience there starts the special contact between the baby's face, mouth, and hands, and her breasts.

One hears of the young mother who is bewildered. Nothing is explained to her; the baby is kept away in another room, perhaps along with other babies, except at feed-times. There is always a baby crying, so that the mother never gets to know the cry of her own baby. At feed-times the babies are brought in and handed to their mothers, wrapped round tightly with a towel. The mother is supposed to take this queer-looking object and breast-feed it (I say 'it' on purpose), but neither does she feel the life welling up in her breasts, nor does the baby have a chance to explore, and to have ideas. One even hears of so-called helpers who get exasperated when the baby does not start sucking, and who push the baby's nose in it, so to speak. There will be a few who have had this sort of horrid experience.

But even mothers have to learn how to be motherly by experience. I think it is much better if they look at it in that way. By experience they grow. If they look at it the other way and think that they must work hard at books to learn how to be perfect mothers from the beginning, they will be on the wrong tack. In the long run, what we need is mothers, as well as fathers, who have found out how to believe in themselves. These mothers and their husbands build the best homes in which babies can grow and develop.

Chapter 8

Breast Feeding

Whereas in the last chapter breast feeding was discussed in a personal way, in this chapter the same subject is treated more technically. First we get to know from the mother's angle what is to be discussed, and then doctors and nurses can work out among themselves what problems mothers may meet and want to ask about.

In a discussion among children's doctors it was pointed out that we do not actually know what is the particular value of breast feeding. Nor do we know what principle should govern us in our choice of the time to wean. Obviously both physiology and psychology have a place in the answering of these questions. We must leave the paediatricians the very complex study of the bodily processes while attempting to make a comment from the point of view of psychology.

Although the psychology of breast feeding is an extremely complex matter probably enough is already known for something clear and helpful to be written. But there is a complication. What is written is not necessarily acceptable, even if it is true. This paradox must first be dealt with.

It is not possible for an adult or even for a child to know exactly what it feels like to be an infant. The feelings of infancy, although no doubt stored up somewhere in every one, are not easily recaptured. The intensity of infant feelings recurs in the intensity of the suffering associated with psychotic symptoms. The infant's preoccupation with feelings of a certain type, at a certain moment, reappears in the ill person's preoccupation with fear or grief. When we observe an infant directly we find it difficult to translate what we see and hear into terms of feeling; or else we imagine, and as likely as not imagine wrongly, because we bring to the situation all sorts of ideas that belong to later development. Mothers who are caring for their own infants come nearest to a true appreciation of infant feelings because of their special ability, which they lose after a few months, to be identified with the infant that is in their special care. But mothers are seldom wanting to communicate what they know until they have forgotten the vital parts of the story.

Doctors and nurses, who are skilled in their own job, are certainly not better than other people at knowing what infants are like as human beings only just launched on the immense task of becoming themselves. It is said that there is nothing in human relationships that is more powerful than the bond between a baby and the mother (or the breast) during the excitement of a breast-feeding experience. I cannot expect this to be easily believed; nevertheless it is necessary at least to have the *possibility* of this in mind when considering such a problem as the value of breast feeding as compared with bottle feeding. It is true of dynamic psychology in general, but particularly of the psychology of early infancy, that the truth of truths cannot be fully and immediately felt. In other sciences if something is found to be true it can usually be accepted without emotional strain, but in psychology there is always this matter of strain, so that something which is not quite true is more easily accepted than the truth itself.

With this preliminary I would make the bald statement that the relation of the infant to the mother during the breast-feeding orgy is especially intense. Also this relationship is complex, for it has to include the excitement of anticipation, the experience of activity during the feed, as well as the sense of gratification, with rest from instinctual tension resulting from satisfaction. At a later age the sexual group of feelings will rival those that belong to breast feeding of infancy, and the individual will be reminded of the latter when experiencing the former, indeed, the pattern of sexual experience will be found to have derived characteristics and peculiarities from the early infantile instinctual life.

Instinctual moments are not the whole thing, however. There is also the infant's relationship with the mother in the periods in between the orgies of feeding, and excretory experiences which have excitement in them and a climax. There is a tremendous task for the infant in early emotional development, in the bringing together of the two types of relationship to the mother; the one in which instinct is roused, and the other in which the mother is the environment and the provider of the ordinary physical necessities of security, warmth, and freedom from the unpredictable.

Nothing so clearly and satisfactorily establishes the infant's conception of the mother as a whole human being as good experiences during excitement, with gratification and satisfaction. As the infant gradually knows the mother as a whole human being there becomes available a technique for giving her something in return for what she has supplied. The infant thus becomes a total human being too, with a capacity to hold the moment of concern, where something is owed but payment has not yet been made. This is the point of origin of the sense of guilt, and of the infant's capacity to feel sad if the loved mother is away. If a mother succeeds doubly in her relationship to her infant, by establishing satisfactory breast feeding and at the same time by remaining the one person in the infant's life over a period of time until both she and the infant can be felt to be whole human beings, then the emotional development of the infant has gone a long way towards the healthy development which forms the basis eventually for independent existence in a world of human beings. Many mothers feel that they do establish contact with their infants within the first few days, and certainly a baby may be expected after a few weeks to give recognition with a smile. All these things are achievements based on good experiences in maternal care, and in the giving of instinctual gratification; at the beginning these achievements can be lost either by feeding hazards, or difficulties in relation to other instinctual experiences, or else by environmental variability that is beyond the infant's capacity for understanding. The early establishment of the whole human relationships, and the maintenance of these, is of the very greatest value in the development of the child.

It is true, undoubtedly, that a mother who for some reason or other is unable to give breast milk is able to carry through most of this early establishment of a human relationship, giving instinctual gratification at the moments of feeding excitement by the use of a bottle. Nevertheless, by and large, it would appear that mothers who are able to feed by the breast are able to find a much richer experience for themselves in the act of feeding, and this seems to contribute to the early establishment of the relationship as between two human beings. If instinctual gratification were alone the clue then there would be no advantage of breast feeding over bottle feeding. There is, however, the whole attitude of the mother which is of paramount importance.

Further, there is a complication which is of extreme importance in the study of the particular value of breast feeding; *the human infant has ideas*. Every function is elaborated in the psyche, and even at the beginning there is fantasy belonging to the excitement and the experience of feeding. The fantasy, such as it is, is of a ruthless attack on the breast, and eventually on the mother, as the infant becomes able to perceive that it is the mother whose breast is attacked. There is a very strong aggressive element in the primitive love impulse which is the feeding impulse. In terms of the fantasy of a slightly later date the mother is ruthlessly attacked, and although but little aggression may be observable it is not possible to ignore the destructive element in the aim of the infant. Satisfactory feeding finishes off the orgy physically, and also rounds off the fantasy experience; nevertheless there develops a considerable degree of concern on account of the aggressive ideas as soon as the infant begins to put two and two together, and to find that the breast that was attacked and emptied is part of the mother.

The infant who has had a thousand goes at the breast is evidently in a very different condition from the infant who has been fed an equal number of times by the bottle; the survival of the mother is more of a miracle in the first case than in the second. I am not suggesting that there is nothing that the mother who is feeding by bottle can do to meet the situation. Undoubtedly she gets played with by her infant, and she gets the playful bite, and it can be seen that when things are going well the infant almost feels the same as if there is breast feeding. Nevertheless there is a difference. In psychoanalysis, where there is time for a gathering together of all the early roots of the full-blown sexual experience of adults, the analyst gets very good evidence that in a satisfactory breast feed the actual fact of taking from part of the mother's body provides a 'blue-print' for all types of experience in which instinct is involved.

It is a common thing for a baby to be unable to take the breast, not because of any inherent inability, which must be very rare indeed, but because of something which interferes with the mother's capacity to adapt to the baby's needs. Wrong advice to persevere with breast feeding is notoriously disastrous. A transfer to the bottle produces relief, and it frequently happens that a baby who is in difficulties shows no further difficulty after transfer from the mother's breast to the more impersonal method, that is to say with the bottle intervening. This corresponds to the value that some babies can get from being laid in the cot, because the richness of the experience of actually being held was spoiled by the mother's anxieties, or her depression, which inevitably distort the holding process. From the recognition of the infant's relief at weaning from an anxious or depressed mother it should be possible for the student of the subject to arrive at a theoretical understanding of the great importance that comes from the mother's *positive* ability to fulfil her function in this respect. Success is important to the mother, sometimes more important to her than to the infant, but it is certainly important to the infant also.

It is necessary to add at this point that success in breast feeding does not mean that all problems are thereby smoothed out; success means that a very much more intense and rich experience of relationships is embarked upon, and along with this goes a greater rather than a lesser chance for the infant to produce symptoms which indicate that the really important inherent difficulties that belong to life, and to human relationships, are being met. When bottle feeding has to be substituted there is often an easing in all respects, and, in terms of easy management, a doctor may feel that by easing matters all round he is obviously doing something good. But this is looking at life in terms of ill-health and health. Those who care for infants must be able to think in terms of poverty and richness in the personality, which is quite another thing.

In the case of the breast-fed infant there soon develops a capacity for using certain objects as symbols of the breast, and therefore of the mother. The relationship to the mother (both excited and quiet) is represented in the relationship of the infant to the fist, to a thumb or fingers, or to a bit of cloth, or to a soft toy. There is a very gradual process in the displacement of the aim of the infant's feelings, and an object only comes to stand for the breast when the idea of the breast has been incorporated into the child through actual experiences. It might be thought at first that the bottle could be a breast substitute, but this only makes sense if the bottle is introduced as a plaything at an appropriate time when the infant has had breast experiences. The bottle given instead of the breast, or substituted in the first weeks, has to be a thing on its own account, and to some extent it represents a barrier between the infant and the mother rather than a link. On the whole, bottles are not good breast substitutes.

It is interesting to examine the subject of weaning as it is affected by the alternatives of breast and bottle feeding. Fundamentally the process of weaning must be the same in the two cases. There arrives a stage in an infant's growth at which there is a play of dropping things, and the mother knows that the infant is reaching a state of development at which weaning can be meaningful to him. In this respect there is a readiness for the weaning, no matter whether the breast or the bottle is being used. To some extent, however, no baby is ever ready to be weaned, and this can be said in spite of the fact that in practice a proportion of babies wean themselves. There is always some anger associated with weaning, and it is here that the breast and the bottle are so different. In the case of the child who is breast-fed the baby and the mother have to negotiate a period in which there is anger with the breast, and in which there are ideas of an attack not so much motivated by desire as by rage. It is obviously a very much richer experience for the infant and mother to come through this successfully than for them to come through the more mechanical feeding technique, with a bottle as a breast substitute. In the experience of weaning it is an important fact that the mother survives all the feelings belonging to weaning, and she survives partly because the infant protects her, and partly because she can protect herself.

There is a practical problem which assumes great importance in some cases in which a child is to be adopted. Is it better for an infant to have the breast for a little while or not at all? I think the answer to this is not available. In the present state of our knowledge we are not certain whether to advise a mother of an illegitimate baby to feed her baby at the breast or to start off with a bottle, when she knows that an adoption is being arranged. It is held by many that a mother feels very much better about handing over her baby if she has had the chance to give breast feeding, at any rate for a certain length of time; but on the other hand she can be extremely distressed at parting with her infant after such a period. This is a very complex problem, because it may be better for a mother to experience the distress rather than to find afterwards that she was cheated of an experience which she would have welcomed, because it was real. Each case has to be treated on its own merits, with due regard to the feelings of the mother. With regard to the baby, it seems clear that successful breast feeding and weaning provides a good basis for adoption, but it is comparatively rare for a child who is started off so well to be adopted. Much more frequently the beginning of the child's life is *muddled*, so that those who are adopting find themselves with a baby in their care who is already disturbed by having had a complex early history. One thing is certain, that these things do matter very much, and that it is not possible when adopting to ignore the feeding history and the history of general management in the first days and weeks. Processes that are started off easily at those times when all goes well may be very difficult indeed to establish a few weeks or months later when there has been a muddle.

One can say that if a child eventually comes for a long psychotherapy it is better that there shall have been some contact with the breast at the beginning, as this gives a basis of richness of relationships which may possibly be recaptured in the treatment. Nevertheless, most children do not come for psychotherapy, and indeed it is but seldom that prolonged psychotherapy is available; therefore it may be better, when arranging an adoption, to be contented with the poorer start of a reliable bottle-feeding technique, which, by the very fact that it does not so intimately introduce the mother herself, makes it easier for the infant to feel that there is consistent management in spite of the fact that several people are engaged in the feeding process. It seems quite likely that the baby who is bottle fed from the beginning, although poorer for the experience, or perhaps *because* of being poorer for the experience, is able to be fed by a series of minders without too much muddle, simply because at least the bottle and the feed remain constant. Something must be reliable for the infant at the beginning, otherwise there is no hope that he or she may start well on the road to mental health.

A great deal of work needs to be done in this field of inquiry, and it must be acknowledged that the most fruitful source of new understanding is in long-continued psychoanalysis of all types of cases, normal, neurotic, and psychotic, of children of all ages, as well as adults.

In *summary*, it can be said that it is not possible to pass over the matter of a substitute for breast feeding lightly. In some countries and cultures bottle feeding is the rule, and this fact must affect the cultural pattern of the community. Breast feeding provides the richest experience and is the more satisfactory method from the mother's point of view, if it goes well. From the infant's point of view the survival of the mother and her breast after breast feeding is very much more important than the survival of a bottle, and of a mother who gives from a bottle. Difficulties can arise in the mother and the infant as a result of the richness of the experience of breast feeding, but this can hardly be taken as an argument against it, since the aim in infant care is not simply the avoidance of symptoms. The aim of infant care is not limited to the establishment of health, but includes the provision of conditions for the richest possible experience, with long-term results in increased depth and value in the character and personality of the individual.

Chapter 9

Why Do Babies Cry?

We have considered some very obvious things about your wish to know your baby and your baby's need to be known. Just as babies need mother's milk and warmth, so do they need her love and understanding. If you know your baby you are in a position to give help just when he or she wants it, and as no one can know a baby as well as the mother can – no one but you can be the right person to help him or her. Let us now consider the times when he seems to be especially asking for help – when he cries.

As you know, most babies cry a lot, and you are constantly having to decide whether to let your baby go on crying or to soothe him, or feed him, or to tell father to have a go, or to hand him over lock, stock, and barrel to the woman upstairs who knows all about children, or thinks she does. You probably wish that I could tell you quite simply what to do, but if I did you would say, 'What a fool! There are all sorts of different reasons why babies cry, and you cannot say what to do until you have found out what the crying is about.' Exactly so, and for this reason I am going to try to sort out with you the reasons for crying.

Let us say that there are four kinds of crying, because that is more or less true, and we can hang all that we want to say on these four pegs: Satisfaction, Pain, Rage, Grief. You will be able to see that really I am saying quite ordinary obvious things, the sort of things that every mother of an infant knows naturally though she has not usually tried thinking out how to express what she knows in words.

What I am saying is no more than this, that crying is either giving the baby the feeling that he is exercising his lungs (satisfaction), or else it is a signal of distress (pain), or else it is an expression of anger (rage), or else it is a song of sadness (grief). If you will accept this as a working proposition I can explain just what I mean.

You may think it strange that I should be talking first about crying for satisfaction, almost for pleasure, because anyone would admit that whenever a baby is crying he must be to some extent in distress. Yet I do think that this is really the first thing to be said. We have to recognize that pleasure enters into crying as it does into the exercise of any bodily function, so that a certain amount of crying can sometimes be said to be satisfactory for the infant, whereas less than that amount would not have been enough.

A mother will tell me, 'My baby seldom cries, except just before feeding. Of course he cries for an hour between four and five every day, but I think he likes it. He is not really in trouble, and I let him see I am about but do not especially try to soothe him.'

Sometimes you may hear people saying that a baby ought never to be picked up when he cries. We will deal with them later. But some other people say that a baby should never be allowed to cry. I feel that these people probably tell mothers not to let babies put their fists into their mouths, or suck their thumbs, or use a dummy, or play about at the breast after serious feeding is over. They do not know that babies have (and have to have) their own ways of dealing with their own troubles.

Anyway, babies who seldom cry are not necessarily, because of their not crying, doing better than babies who cry like billy-o, and, personally, if I had to choose between the two extremes, I would bet on the crying baby, who had come to know the full extent of his capacity to make a noise, provided the crying had not been allowed too often to go over into despair.

What I am saying now is that any exercise of the body is good, from the infant's point of view. Breathing itself, a new achievement to the new-born, may be quite interesting until it is taken for granted, and screaming and yelling and all forms of crying must be definitely exciting. The importance of our recognizing this, the value of crying, is that we can then see how crying works as a reassurance in time of trouble. Babies cry because they feel anxious or insecure, and it works; the crying helps a lot, and we must therefore agree that there is something good about it. Later comes talking, and in time the toddler will be banging on a drum.

You know how your infant uses his fist or his finger, how he pushes it into his mouth and so manages to stand frustration. Well, screaming is like a fist that comes up from inside. And no one can interfere. You can hold your baby's hands away from his mouth, but you cannot pin his crying down into his stomach. You cannot altogether stop your baby from crying and I hope you will not try. If you have neighbours who cannot stand the noise, you are unlucky, because then you have to take steps to stop the crying on account of *their* feelings, which is a different thing from studying the reasons why your baby cries, so as to be able to prevent or stop only the crying that is unhelpful and possibly harmful.

Doctors say that the lusty cry of the new-born infant is a sign of health and strength. Well, crying goes on being a sign of health and strength, an early form of P.T., an exercise of a function, satisfying as such, and even pleasurable. *But it is very much more than this,* so now what about the other meanings of crying?

No one will find it in the least difficult to recognize the cry of pain, nature's way of letting you know your baby is in trouble and needs your help.

When a baby is in pain he utters a shrill or piercing sound, and often at the same time gives some indication of where the trouble lies. For instance, if he has colic, he draws up his legs; if it is ear-ache, he puts a hand up towards the bad ear; if it is a bright light that is worrying him he may turn his head away. He does not know what to do about loud bangs.

The cry of pain is not in itself pleasurable to the infant and no one would think it was, because it immediately awakes in the people around the urge to do something about it.

One kind of pain is called hunger. Yes, I think hunger does seem like a pain to the infant. Hunger hurts him in a way that is apt to be forgotten by grown-ups, who quite seldom get hungry painfully. In the British Isles today I suppose very few know what it is to be painfully hungry. Think of all that we do to ensure a supply of food, even in wartime. We wonder what we shall eat, but we seldom wonder whether we shall eat. And if we are short of something we like, we go off it and stop wanting it, rather than go on wanting it and not getting it. But our infants know only too well the pains and pangs of acute hunger. Mothers like their infants to be nice and greedy, to get excited as they hear the noise, and see the sights, and smell the smells that advertise the fact that food is due; and excited babies are feeling pain and show it by crying. This pain is soon forgotten if it leads to satisfactory feeding.

The cry of pain is something that we hear any time after the baby's birth. Sooner or later we notice a new kind of painful crying, the crying of apprehension. I think that this means that the baby is getting to know a thing or two. He has come to know that in certain circumstances he must *expect* pain. As you start to undress him he knows he is to be taken out of comfortable warmth, he knows his position will be changed this way and that, and that all feeling of security will be lost, and so he cries as you undo his top button. He has put two and two together, he has had experiences, and one thing reminds him of another. Naturally all this becomes more and more complex as the weeks go by, and as he gets older.

As you know, a baby sometimes cries when he is dirty. This might mean that the baby does not like being dirty (and, of course, if he remains dirty long enough his skin will become chafed and hurt him), but usually it means nothing of the kind – it means that he fears the disturbance he has learned to expect. Experience has shown him that the next few minutes will bring about a failure of all the reassurances, that is to say he will be uncovered, and moved, and he will lose heat.

The basis of the crying of fear is pain, and that is why the crying sounds the same in each case, but it is pain remembered and expected to recur. After a baby has experienced any painfully acute feelings he may cry from fear when anything happens which threatens to make him have those feelings again. And quite soon he begins to develop ideas, some of them frightening, and here again, if he cries, the trouble is that something is reminding the baby of pain, although that something is imaginary.

If you have only just started thinking about these things it may seem to you that I am making it all rather difficult and complicated, but I cannot help it and, fortunately, the next bit is as easy as winking, for the third cause of crying on my list is rage.

We all know what it is like to lose our tempers and we all know how anger, when it is very intense, sometimes seems to possess us so that we cannot for the time being control ourselves. Your baby knows about being all-out angry. However much you try, you will disappoint him at times, and he will cry in anger; according to my view you have one consolation – that angry crying probably means that he has some belief in you. He hopes he may change you. A baby who has lost belief does not get angry, he just stops wanting, or else he cries in a miserable, disillusioned way, or else he starts banging with his head on the pillow, or on the wall or the floor, or else he exploits the various things he can do with his body.

It is a healthy thing for a baby to get to know the full extent of his rage. You see, he certainly will not *feel* harmless when he is angry. You know what he looks like. He screams and kicks and, if he is old enough, he stands up and shakes the bars of the cot. He bites and scratches, and he may spit and spew and make a mess. If he really is determined he can hold his breath and go blue in the face, and even have a fit. For a few minutes he really intends to destroy or at least to spoil everyone and everything, and he does not even mind if he destroys himself in the process. Naturally you do what you can to get the child out of this state. It can be said, however, that if a baby cries in a state of rage and feels as if he has destroyed everyone and everything, and yet the people round him remain calm and unhurt, this experience greatly strengthens his ability to see that what he feels to be true is not necessarily real, that fantasy and fact, both important, are nevertheless different from each other. There is absolutely no need for you to try to make him angry, for the simple reason that there are plenty of ways in which you cannot help making him angry whether you like it or not.

Some people go about the world terrified of losing their tempers, afraid of what would have happened if they had experienced rage to the fullest extent when they were infants. For some reason or other this never got properly tested out. Perhaps their mothers were scared. By calm behaviour they might have given confidence, but they muddled things up by acting as if the angry baby was really dangerous.

A baby in a rage is very much a person. He knows what he wants, he knows how he might get it, and he refuses to give up hope. At first he hardly knows that he has weapons. At first he can scarcely know that his yells hurt, any more than he knows that his messes give trouble. But in the course of a few months he begins to feel dangerous and to feel he can hurt and to feel he wants to hurt; and sooner or later, from personal experience of pain, he gets to know that others can suffer pain and get tired.

You can get much interest out of watching your infant for the first signs that he knows he can hurt you, and that he intends to hurt you.

Now I want to get down to the fourth on the list of the causes of crying – grief. I know that I do not have to describe sadness to you, any more than I should have to describe colour to someone not suffering from colour blindness. Yet it is not good enough for me just to mention sadness and leave it at that, for various reasons. One is that the feelings of infants are very direct and intense, and we grown-ups, although we value these intense feelings of our infancy, and like to recapture them at chosen times, have learned long since how to defend ourselves from being at the mercy of almost unbearable feelings, such as we were liable to as babies. If by the loss of someone we love deeply we cannot avoid painful grief, we just settle down to a period of mourning, which our friends understand and tolerate. And from this we may be expected sooner or later to recover. We do not just lay ourselves open to acute grief at any moment of the day or night as babies do. In fact many people defend themselves against painful grief so well that they cannot take things as seriously as they would like to take them; they cannot feel the deep feelings which they would like to feel, because they are afraid of anything so real. And they find themselves unable to take the risks involved in loving a definite person or thing; spreading their risks they may lose a lot, though they gain through being well insured against grief. How people love a sad film that makes them shed tears, which shows at least that they have not lost the art! When I talk about grief as a cause of infant crying I have to remind you that you will not easily remember the grief that belongs to your own infancy, and that therefore you will not be able to believe in your own infant's grief by direct sympathy.

Even babies can develop powerful defences against painful sadness. But I am trying to describe to you the sad crying of infants which does exist, and which you have almost certainly heard. I should like to be able to help you to see the place of sad crying and its meaning and value, so that you may know what to do when you hear it.

I am suggesting to you that when your infant shows that he can cry from sadness you can infer that he has travelled a long way in the development of his feelings; and yet I am saying, as I said about rage, that you would gain nothing by *trying to cause* sad crying. You will not be able to help making him sad any more than you can help making him angry. But there is a difference here between rage and grief, because whereas rage is a more or less direct reaction to frustration, grief implies quite complex goings-on in the infant's mind, which I will try to describe.

But first a word about the sound of sad crying, which I think you will agree has a musical note in it. Some people think that sad crying is one of the main roots of the more valuable kind of music. And by sad crying an infant to some extent entertains himself. He may easily develop and experiment with the various tones of his crying while he is waiting for sleep to come to drown his sorrows. A little older, and he will be actually heard sadly singing himself to sleep. Also, as you know, tears belong more to sad crying than to rage, and inability to cry sadly means dry eyes and a dry nose (into which the tears flow when they do not dribble down the face). So tears are healthy, both physically and psychologically.

Perhaps I could give an illustration to explain to you what I mean about the value of sadness. I will take an eighteen-month-old child because it is easier to believe in what happens at this age than in the same things happening more obscurely in earlier infancy. This little girl had been adopted at four months and had had unfortunate experiences before adoption, and for this reason was specially dependent on her mother. One could say that she had not been able to build up in her mind, as well as more fortunate babies are able to do, the idea that there are good mothers about; and for this reason she clung to the actual person of her adoptive mother, who was excellent in her care of her. The child's need of the actual presence of her adoptive mother was so great that the mother knew she must not leave the child. When the infant was seven months old she had once left her in excellent hands for half a day, but the result was nearly disastrous. Now, when the child was eighteen months old, the mother decided to take a fortnight's holiday, telling the child all about it, and leaving her in the hands of people she knew well. The child spent most of the fortnight trying the handle of her mother's bedroom door, too anxious to play, and not really accepting the fact of her mother's absence. She was much too frightened to be sad. I suppose one would say that, for her, the world stood still for a fortnight. When at last the mother came back, the child waited a little while to make sure that what she saw was real, and then she flung her arms around her mother's neck and lost herself in sobbing and deep sadness, after which she returned to her normal state.

You see how the sadness was there before the mother came back, looking at it from our point of view as outsiders. But from the little girl's point of view there was no sadness until she knew she could be sad with her mother there, her tears dropping down on to her mother's neck. Why should this be so? Well, I think we may have to say that this little girl had to cope with something which frightened her very much, that is to say with the hate of her mother that she felt when her mother left her. I chose this illustration because the fact that the child was dependent on her adoptive mother (and could not easily find motherliness in other people) makes it easy for us to see how dangerous the child would feel it to be to hate her mother. So she waited till her mother came back.

But what did she do when the mother came back? She might have gone up to her and bitten her. I should not be at all surprised if some of you have had such an experience. But this child flung her arms round her mother's neck and sobbed. What was mother to understand by this? If she had put it into words, which I am glad to say she did not, she would have said, 'I am your only good mother. You were frightened to find you hated me for going away. You are sorry you hated me. Not only that, you felt that I went away because of something bad you had done, or because you made such great demands on me, or because you hated me before I went; so you felt that you were the cause of my going away – you felt I was gone for ever. It was not till I was back and you had your arms round my neck that you could acknowledge that you had it in you to send me away, even while I was with you. By your sadness you earned the right to put your arms round my neck, because you showed that you felt that when I hurt you by going away it was your fault. In fact, you felt guilty, as if you were the cause of everything bad in the world, whereas really you were only a little bit the cause of my going away. Babies are a trouble, but mothers expect them to be and like them to be. Through being extra dependent on me you have been extra liable to tire me out; but I chose to adopt you, and I never feel resentment at being tired out by you . . .'

She might have said all this, but, thank goodness, she did not; as a matter of fact these ideas never entered her mind. She was much too busy cuddling her little girl.

Why have I said all these things about a little girl's sobbing? I am sure no two people would describe what is going on when a child is sad in the same way, and I dare say that some of what I said is not quite rightly put. But it is not all wrong, and I am hoping that by what I have said I have been able to show you that sad crying is something very complicated, something which means that your infant has already gained his place in the world. He is no longer a cork floating on the waves. He has already started to take responsibility for environment. Instead of just reacting to circumstances he has come to feel responsible for the circumstances. The trouble is that he starts off feeling *totally* responsible for what happens to him and for the external factors in his life. Only gradually does he sort out what he *is* responsible for from all that he *feels* responsible for.

Now let us compare sad crying with the other kinds. You can see that crying from pain and hunger can be noted any time from birth onwards. Rage appears as the infant becomes able to put two and two together, and fear, indicating pain expected, means that the baby has developed ideas. Grief indicates something far in advance of these other acute feelings; and if mothers understand how valuable the things are underlying sadness they will be able to avoid missing something important. People easily find themselves glad later on when their child says 'Thank you' and 'I am sorry', but the earlier version of this is contained in the infant's sad crying, and this is much more valuable than what is taught in the way of the expression of gratitude and repentance.

You will have noted in my description of the sad little girl how it was perfectly logical for her to be sad on her mother's neck. An angry baby would scarcely be expected to be angry while in a satisfactory relation to mother. If he stayed on her lap it would be because he was afraid to leave it, and mother would probably wish he would go away. But the sad baby can be taken and cuddled because, by his taking responsibility for what hurts him, he earns the right to keep a good relation to people. In fact a sad baby may *need* your physical and demonstrative love. What he does not need, however, is to be jogged and tickled, and in other ways distracted from his sadness. Let us say he is in a state of mourning and requires a certain length of time to recover from it. He just needs to know that you continue to love him, and it may even be best sometimes to let him lie crying on his own. Remember that there is no better feeling in infancy or childhood than that which belongs to true spontaneous recovery from sadness and guilt feelings. This is so true that sometimes you will find your child being naughty so as to feel guilty and cry, and then feel forgiven, so eager is he to recapture what he has experienced in true recovery from sadness.

So now I have described various kinds of crying. There is so very much more to be said. But I think you may have been helped by my attempt to sort out one kind from another. What I have not done is to describe the crying of hopelessness and despair, the crying that the other kinds break down into if there is no hope left in the baby's mind. In your home you may never hear this kind of crying, and if you do the situation has got beyond you, and you are in need of help, although, as I have tried to make especially clear, you are otherwise much better than any one else can be in the management of your own infant. It is in institutions that we hear the crying of hopelessness and disintegration, where there is no means of providing one mother for each baby. I only mention this kind of crying for the sake of completeness. The fact that you are willing to devote yourself to the care of your infant means that he is lucky; unless something should happen by chance to upset your routine management he will be able to go straight ahead, letting you know when he is angry with you and when he loves you, and when he wants to be rid of you, and when he is anxious or frightened, and when he just wants you to understand that he is experiencing sadness.

Chapter 10

The World in Small Doses

If you listen to philosophical discussions you sometimes hear people using a lot of words over the business of what is real and what is not real. One person says that real means what we can all touch, see, and hear, while another says that it is only what feels real that counts, like a nightmare, or hating the man who jumps the bus queue. This sounds all very difficult. What relevance can these things have for the mother looking after her baby? I hope I will be able to explain.

Mothers with babies are dealing with a developing, changing situation; the baby starts off not knowing about the world, and by the time they have finished their job the baby is grown up into someone who knows about the world and can find a way to live in it, and even to take part in the way it behaves. What a tremendous development!

But you will know people who have difficulties in their relation to the things that we call real. They do not feel them to be real. For you and me things feel more real sometimes than at other times. Any one may have a dream that feels more real than reality, and for some people their personal imaginative world is so much more real to them than what we call the real world that they cannot make a good job of living in the world at all.

Now let us ask the question, why is it that the ordinary healthy person has at one and the same time a feeling of the realness of the world, and of the realness of what is imaginative and personal? How did it come about that you and I are like that? It is a great advantage to be like that, because if we are we can use our imagination to make the world more exciting, and we can use the things of the real world to be imaginative about. Do we just grow like that? Well, what I am saying is that we do not grow like that, not unless at the beginning each one of us has a mother able to introduce the world to us in small doses.

Now what are children like when they are two, three, or four years old? In this particular matter of seeing the world as it is, what can we say about the toddler? For the toddler, every sensation is tremendously intense. We, as grown-ups, only at special moments reach this wonderful intensity of feeling which belongs to the early years, and anything that helps us to get there without frightening us is welcome. For some it is music or a picture that gets us there, for some it is a football match, and for others it is dressing up for a dance, or getting a glimpse of the Queen as she passes in her car. Happy are those whose feet are well planted on the earth and yet who keep the capacity for enjoying intense sensations, even if only in the dreams that are dreamed and remembered.

For the little child, and how much more for the infant, life is just a series of terrifically intense experiences. You have noticed what happens when you interrupt play; in fact you like to give warning, so that if possible the child will be able to bring the play to some sort of an end and so tolerate your interference. A toy that an uncle gave your little boy is a bit of the real world, and yet if it is given in the right way at the right time and by the right person it has a meaning for the child which we ought to be able to understand and allow for. Perhaps we can remember a little toy that we had ourselves, and what it meant to us then. How drab it looks now if it is still on the mantelpiece! The child of two, three, and four is in two worlds at once. The world that we share with the child is also the child's own imaginative world, and so the child is able to experience it intensely. The reason for this is that we do not insist, when we are dealing with a child of that age, on an exact perception of the external world. A child's feet need not be all the time firmly planted on the earth. If a little girl wants to fly we do not just say 'Children don't fly'. Instead of that we pick her up and carry her around above our heads and put her on top of the cupboard, so that she feels she has flown like a bird to her nest.

Only too soon the child will find that flying cannot be done magically. Probably in dreams magical floating through the air may be retained to some extent, or at any rate there will be a dream about taking rather long steps. Some fairy story like the one about the Seven-League Boots, or the Magic Carpet, will be the grown-ups' contribution to this theme. At ten years or so the child will be practising long-jump and high-jump, trying to jump farther and higher than the others. That will be all that remains, except dreams, of the tremendously acute sensations associated with the idea of flying that came naturally at the age of three.

The point is that we don't clamp down reality on the little child, and we hope that we shall not have to clamp it down even when the child is five or six years old, because, if all goes well, by that age the child will have started a scientific interest in this thing that grown-ups call the real world. This real world has much to offer, as long as its acceptance does not mean a loss of the reality of the personal imaginative or inner world.

For the little child it is legitimate for the inner world to be outside as well as inside, and we therefore enter into the imaginative world of the child when we play the child's games and take part in other ways in the child's imaginative experiences.

Here is a little boy of three. He is happy, he plays all day long on his own or with other children, and he is able to sit up at table and eat like grown-up people. In the day-time he is getting quite good at knowing the difference between what we call real things and what we call the child's imagination. What is he like in the night? He sleeps, and no doubt dreams. Sometimes he wakes with a piercing yell. Mother jumps out of bed and goes in and turns on the light, and makes to take the child up in her arms. Is he pleased? On the contrary; he screams, 'Go away, you witch! I want my mummy'. His dream world has spread into what we call the actual world, and for twenty minutes or so the mother waits, unable to do anything, because for the child she is a witch. Suddenly he puts his arms round her neck and clings to her as if she had only just turned up, and before he is able to tell her about the broomstick he drops off to sleep, so that his mother is able to put him back in the cot and return to her own bed.

What about a seven-year-old little girl, a nice little child, who tells you that at her new school all the children are against her, and the mistress is horrid and is always picking her out, making an example of her and humiliating her? Of course you go to the school and have a talk with the teacher. I am not suggesting that all teachers are perfect; nevertheless you may find she is quite a straightforward person, and that, in fact, it distresses her that this child seems to bring troubles on herself.

Well, here again you know what children are. They are not supposed to know exactly what the world is like. They must be allowed to have what would be called delusions if we were talking about grown-ups. Probably you solve the whole problem by asking the teacher to tea. Soon you may find the child going to the other extreme, and having a very strong attachment to the teacher, even idolizing her, and now fearing the other children because of the teacher's love. In the course of time the whole thing settles down.

Now, if we look at smaller children at a nursery school it is hard to guess whether they will like their teacher from what we know about her. You might know her, and perhaps you do not think much of her. She's not attractive. She acted rather selfishly when her mother was ill, or something. What the child feels about her is not based on that sort of thing. It may be that the child becomes dependent on her, and is devoted to her, because she is reliably there and kind, and she may easily become someone who is necessary for the child's happiness and growth.

But all this comes out of the relationship that exists earlier between the mother and the infant. Here there are special conditions. The mother is sharing a specialized bit of the world with her small child, keeping that bit small enough so that the child is not muddled, yet enlarging it very gradually so that the growing capacity of the child to enjoy the world is catered for. This is one of the most important parts of her job. She does it naturally.

If we look more carefully at this we shall see that there are two things that a mother does which help here. One is that she takes the trouble to avoid coincidences. Coincidences lead to muddle. Examples would be handing a baby over to someone else's care at the same time as weaning, or introducing solids during an attack of measles, and so on. The other thing is that she is able to distinguish between fact and fantasy. This is worth looking at a bit more closely.

When the boy woke up in the night and called his mother a witch, she was quite clear that she was not a witch, and so she was content to wait until he came round. When the next day he asked her, 'Are there really witches, mummy?' she quite easily said 'No'. At the same time she looked out a story book with a witch in it. When your little boy turns away from the milk pudding you have specially prepared with the very best ingredients, and makes a face intended to convey the idea that it is poisonous, you are not upset, because you know perfectly well that it is good. You also know that just for the moment he feels that it is poisonous. You find ways round the difficulty, and quite possibly in a few minutes the pudding will be eaten with relish. If you had been uncertain of yourself you would have got all fussed up, and would have tried to force the pudding into the child's mouth to prove to *yourself* that it was good.

In all sorts of ways your clear knowledge of what is real and what is not real helps the child, because the child is only gradually getting to the understanding that the world is not as imagined, and that imagination is not exactly like the world. Each needs the other. You know that first object your baby loves – a bit of blanket or a soft toy – for the infant this is almost part of the self, and if it is taken away or washed the result is disaster. As the baby becomes able to start throwing this and other things away (expecting them to be picked up and returned, of course), you know the time is coming when you can begin to be allowed by your infant to go away and return.

I want to get back now to the beginnings. These later things are easy if the beginning happens to go well. I would like to look at the early feeding again. You remember I was describing the way in which the mother makes her breast available (or the bottle) just as the baby is preparing to conjure up something, and then lets it disappear as the idea of it fades from the baby's mind. Do you see how in doing this she is making a good start with the introduction of the world to the baby? In nine months the mother gives about a thousand feeds, and look at all the other things she does with the same delicate adaptation to exact needs. For the lucky infant the world starts off behaving in such a way that it joins up with his imagination, and so the world is woven into the texture of the imagination, and the inner life of the baby is enriched with what is perceived in the external world.

And now let us look again at the people talking about what 'real' means. If one of them had a mother who introduced the world to him when he was a baby in the ordinary good way, as you have been introducing the world to your own baby, then he will be able to see that real means two things, and he will be able to feel both kinds of reality at once. Next to him may be another person whose mother made a mess of it all, and for whom there has to be either one kind of real, or the other kind. For this unfortunate man either the world is there and everyone sees the same thing, or else everything is imaginary and personal. We can leave these two people arguing.

So a great deal depends on the way the world is presented to the infant and to the growing child. The ordinary mother can start and carry through this amazing business of introducing the world in small doses, not because she is clever, as philosophers need to be, but simply because of the devotion she feels for her own baby.

Chapter 11

The Baby as a Person

I have been wondering how to start to describe babies as persons. It is easy to see that when food goes into the baby it is digested, and some of it is distributed round the body and used for growth. Some of it is stored as energy, and some of it is got rid of in one way or another. That is looking at the baby with an interest in bodies. But if we look at the same baby, being interested in the person that is there, we can easily see that there is an imaginative feeding experience, as well as this bodily one. The one is based on the other.

I think you can get quite a lot out of thinking that all the things that you do because of your love of the baby go in just like the food. The baby builds something out of it all, and not only that, but the baby has phases of making use of you and then dropping you, just in the same way as with the food. Perhaps I can explain what I mean best by letting him suddenly grow up a little.

Here is a ten-month-old baby boy. He is sitting on his mother's knee while the mother is talking to me. He is lively and awake, and naturally interested in things. Instead of just letting everything get into a muddle I place an attractive object on the corner of the table, between where I am sitting and where the mother is sitting. The mother and I can go on talking, but out of the corner of one eye we can watch the baby. You may be sure that if he is just an ordinary baby he will notice the attractive object (let us call it a spoon), and he will reach for it. As a matter of fact, probably as soon as he has reached for it, he will suddenly be overcome with reserve. It is as if he thought, 'I had better think this thing out: I wonder what feelings mother will have on this subject. I had better hold back until I know.' So he will turn away from the spoon as if nothing were further from his thoughts. In a few moments, however, he will return to his interest in it, and he will very tentatively put a finger on the spoon. He may perhaps grasp it, and look at mother to see what he can get from her eyes. At this point I will probably have to tell mother what to do, because otherwise she will help too much, or hinder, as the case may be; so I ask her to play as small a part in what happens as possible.

He gradually finds from his mother's eyes that this new thing he is doing is not disapproved of, and so he catches hold of the spoon more firmly and begins to make it his own. He is still very tense, however, because he is not certain what will happen if he does with this thing what he wants to do so badly. He does not even know for sure what it is that he wants to do.

We guess that in the course of a little while he will discover what he wants to do with it, because his mouth begins to get excited. He is still very quiet and thoughtful, but saliva begins to flow from his mouth. His tongue looks sloppy. His mouth begins to want the spoon. His gums begin to want to enjoy biting on it. It is not very long before he has put it in his mouth. Then he has feelings about it in the ordinary aggressive way that belongs to lions and tigers, and babies, when they get hold of something good. He makes as if to eat it.

We can now say that the baby has taken this thing and made it his own. He has lost all the stillness that belongs to concentration, and wondering, and doubt. Instead he is confident, and very much enriched by the new acquisition. I would say that in imagination he has eaten it. Just as the food goes in and is digested and becomes part of him, so this which has been made his own in an imaginative way is now part of himself and can be used. How will it be used?

Well, you know the answer because this is only a special case of what is going on all the time at home. He will put it to mother's mouth to feed her, and he will want her to play at eating it. Mind you, he does not want her to bite it really, and he would be rather frightened if she actually let it go into her mouth. It's a game; it is an exercise of the imagination. He is playing, and he invites play. What else will he do? He will feed me, and he may want me to play at eating it too. He may make a gesture towards the mouth of someone on the other side of the room. Let everybody share this good thing. He has had it; why shouldn't everyone have it? He has something he can be generous with. Now he puts it inside his mother's blouse where her breast is, and then rediscovers it and takes it out again. Now he shoves it under the blotting pad and enjoys the game of losing it and finding it again, or he notices a bowl on the table and starts scooping imaginary food out of the bowl, imaginatively eating his broth. The experience is a rich one. It corresponds to the mystery of the middle of the body, the digestive processes, the time between when the food is lost by being swallowed, and when the residue is rediscovered at the lower end in the faeces and urine. I could go on for a long time describing how different babies show that they are enriched by this kind of playing.

Now the baby has dropped the spoon. I suppose his interest began to get transferred on to something else. I will pick it up and he can take it again. Yes, he seems to want it, and he takes up the game again, using the spoon as before, as an extra bit of himself. Oh, he's dropped it again! Evidently it was not quite by chance that he dropped it. Perhaps he likes the sound of the spoon as it falls on the floor. We will see. I will hand it to him again. Now he just takes it and drops it quite deliberately; dropping it is what he wants to do. Once again I give it back to him, and he practically throws it away. He is now reaching out for other interests, the spoon is finished with; we have come to the end of the show.

We have watched the baby develop an interest in something, and make it part of himself, and we have watched him use it, and then finish with it. This sort of thing is going on all the time at home, but the sequence is more obvious in this special setting, which gives time for the baby to go right through an experience.

What have we learned watching this little baby boy?

For one thing, we have witnessed a completed experience. Because of the controlled circumstances there could be a beginning, a middle, and an end to what happened; there was a total happening. *This is good for the baby.* When you are in a hurry, or are harassed, you cannot allow for *total happenings*, and your baby is the poorer. When you have time, however, as you certainly should have when you have care of a baby, you can allow for these. Total happenings enable babies to catch hold of time. They do not start off knowing that when something is on it will finish.

Do you see how the middle of things can be enjoyed (or if bad, tolerated) only if there is a strong sense of start and finish?

By allowing your baby time for total experiences, and by taking part in them, you gradually lay a foundation for the child's ability eventually to enjoy all sorts of experiences without jumpiness.

Another thing we can get out of watching that baby with the spoon. We saw how there came doubt and hesitation at the start of a new venture. We watched the child stretch out and touch and handle the spoon, and after the first simple reaction he temporarily withdrew interest. Then, by carefully sensing the feelings of his mother, he allowed interest to return. He was tense and uncertain, however, till he had actually got the spoon to his mouth and had chewed it.

At first your baby is ready to consult you, if you are there when new situations arise. So you will need to know clearly what to let the baby touch, and what not to allow. The simplest way is the best, and this is to avoid having things around that the baby must not take and mouth. You see, the baby is trying to get at the principles that underlie your decisions, so as eventually to be able to foretell what you allow. A little later words will help, and you will say 'too sharp', 'too hot', or in some other way indicate danger to the body; or you will have a way of letting it be known that your engagement ring, put on one side while you are washing, is not put there for the baby's benefit.

Do you see how you can help your baby to avoid being in a muddle about what is good and what is bad to touch? You do this simply by being clear yourself as to what you prohibit, and why; and by being there on the spot, a preventer rather than a curer. Also, you deliberately provide things that the baby will like to handle and chew.

Another thing. We could talk of what we saw in terms of skills, the baby learning to reach out and to find and to grasp, and to put an object to the mouth. I am surprised when a baby of six months goes through this whole performance. On the other hand the interests of a child of fourteen months are too varied for us to expect to see anything so clearly as we saw with our ten-month-old baby boy.

But I think the best thing we learned watching the baby was this. *We saw by what happened that he is not just a body, he is a person.*

The ages at which various kinds of skill develop are interesting to record, but there was more in this than skill. There was play. By playing, the baby showed that he had built up something in himself that could be called material for play, an inner world of imaginative liveliness, which the playing expresses.

Who can say how early there are the beginnings of this imaginative life of the infant, which enriches and is enriched by the bodily experience? At three months a baby may want to put a finger on mother's breast, playing at feeding her, while taking milk at the breast. And what about the earlier weeks? Who knows? A tiny baby may want to suck a fist or finger, while taking from breast or bottle (having cake *and* eating it, so to speak), and this shows that there is something more than just a need for the satisfaction of hunger.

But for whom am I writing? Mothers have no difficulty in seeing the person in their own babies from the start. But there are people who tell you that until they are six months old babies are nothing but bodies and reflexes. Don't be put off by people who talk like that, will you?

Enjoy finding what there is to be found, as it turns up, of the person your baby is, because the baby needs this of you. So you will be ready waiting, without hurry, fuss, or impatience, for the baby's playfulness. It is this, above all, which indicates the existence of a personal inner life in the baby. If it meets in yourself a corresponding playfulness the inner richness of the baby blossoms out, and your playing together becomes the best part of the relationship between the two of you.

Chapter 12

Weaning

You know me well enough by now not to expect me to tell you exactly how and when to wean; there are more good methods than one, and you can get advice from your Health Visitor or clinic. What I want to do is to talk about weaning in a general way, to help you to see what you are doing, whichever way you do it.

The fact is that most mothers don't have any difficulty. Why is this?

The main thing is that the feeding itself has gone well. The baby really has had something to be weaned from. You cannot deprive people of something they have never had.

I can distinctly remember on one occasion, as a little boy, being allowed to eat as much of raspberries and cream as I could possibly take. It was a wonderful experience. Now I can enjoy memories of that one experience better than I enjoy eating raspberries. Perhaps you can remember something like that?

So the basis of weaning is the good feeding experience. In an ordinary nine months at the breast a baby has had it a thousand or so times, and this gives plenty of good memories, or material for good dreams. But it is not the thousand times, it is also the way the baby and the mother were brought together. The mother's sensitive adaptation (as I have said so often) to the infant's needs started off the idea of the world as a good place. The world went to meet the infant, and so the infant could go out to meet the world. The mother's cooperation with the baby at the beginning led naturally on to the baby's cooperation with the mother.

If you believe, as I do, that the baby has ideas right from the start, the feeding times were often pretty terrible, disrupting the quiet of sleep or of waking contemplation. Instinctual demands can be fierce and frightening, and at first can seem to the infant like threats to existence. Being hungry is like being possessed by wolves.

By nine months the baby has become used to this sort of thing, and has become able to hold together even while these instinctual urges hold sway. The baby has even become able to acknowledge the urges as a part of what it means to be a person alive.

As we look at the infant developing into a person, we can see how the mother is gradually perceived in the quiet times as a person too, as something attractive and valued exactly as she appears. How awful then to be hungry, and to feel oneself ruthlessly attacking this same mother. No wonder infants often lose appetite. No wonder some infants fail to allow the breasts to the mother, but separate off the mother who is loved as whole and beautiful from the things (the breasts) that are the objects of excited attack.

Adults find it difficult to let themselves go when they are excited about each other, and this causes much misery, and makes for unsuccessful marriages. The basis for eventual health in this and in many other respects is the whole experience of being carried through infancy by the ordinary good mother who is not afraid of her infant's ideas, and who loves it when her baby goes at her all out.

Perhaps you see why it really is a richer experience for a mother to feed by the breast, and for a baby to be fed at the breast? Everything can be done as well by bottle, and often it is best to go on to the bottle, which may be easier for the baby precisely because it is less exciting. But the breast-feeding experience carried through and terminated successfully is a good basis for life. It provides rich dreams, and makes people able to take risks.

But all good things must come to an end, as the saying is. It is part of the good thing that it ends.

In the last chapter I described a baby who caught hold of a spoon. He took it, he mouthed it, he enjoyed having it to play with and then he dropped it. So the idea of the ending can come from the baby.

It is plain that at seven, eight, or nine months a baby is beginning to be able to play games of throwing things away. It is a very important game, and it can even be exasperating, because someone has to be all the time bringing back the things thrown down. Even in the street, when you come out of the shop you find the baby has thrown out of the pram on to the pavement a teddy-bear, two gloves, a pillow, three potatoes, and a piece of soap. Probably you find someone picking everything up, because the baby obviously expects this.

By nine months most babies are pretty clear about getting rid of things. They may even wean themselves.

In weaning, the aim really is to use the baby's developing ability to get rid of things, and to let the loss of the breast be not just simply a chance affair.

But we must look to see why a baby should ever be weaned at all. Why not go on for ever? Well, I think I have to say that it would be sentimental never to wean. It would be unreal somehow. A wish to wean must come from the mother. She must be brave enough to stand the baby's anger and the awful ideas that go with anger, and just to do what rounds off the job of good feeding. No doubt the baby who has been successfully fed is happy to be weaned in due course, especially as there goes with this a vast extension of the field of experience.

Naturally, when weaning-time comes you will be already introducing other things. You will have provided hard things, rusks and so on, for the baby to chew, and you will have substituted broth or something for one of the breast feeds. You will have put up with a possible refusal of anything new, and found that, by waiting and then going back to the thing that had been refused, you may be rewarded by an acceptance of it. There is usually no need for a sudden change-over from all breast to no breast at all. When (through illness or some other bad chance) the sudden change-over has had to be made, you will have expected difficulties.

If you know that the reactions to weaning are complex you will naturally avoid handing your baby over to someone else's care just as you wean. It would be a pity to wean at the same time as you move from one home to another, or when you go to stay with your aunt. Weaning is one of those experiences that the baby can grow on, if you provide a stable setting for the experience. If you cannot do this, then weaning can be a time when difficulties start.

Another thing, you may easily find that your baby thrives on being weaned in the day, but perhaps for the last feed the breast is the only good thing. You see, your baby is growing up, but his forward march is not maintained all the time. You will find this all along. You will be quite happy if your child is as old as his age some of the time; perhaps he will be beyond his age at certain moments. But every now and again he will be just a baby, even a tiny baby. And you go to meet these changes.

Your older boy is dressing up and bravely fighting enemies. He is ordering everyone about. He bumps his head on the table as he stands up and then suddenly he is a baby, with his head on your lap, sobbing. You expect this, and you expect your baby of twelve months to be only six months old at times. It is all part of your skilled job, knowing just how old your child is at any one moment.

So you may be going on with a breast feed in the evening after you have weaned in the day. But sooner or later you will have to wean altogether, and if you know what you intend to do it is easier for the child than if you cannot make up your mind.

Let me look and see now what reactions you may expect to the weaning which you so bravely do. It may be, as I have said, that the baby does a self-weaning act, and so you do not notice any trouble. Even here there may be some lessening of the zest for food.

Very often, when the weaning is done it is done gradually, and in a stable setting, and no special trouble arises. The infant obviously loves to have the new experience. But I do not want you to think it is very unusual if there are reactions to weaning, even severe ones. A baby who has been doing well may react by losing eagerness for food, or by painfully refusing food, showing a longing for it by irritability and crying. It would be harmful to force food on the baby at this stage. For the time being everything has gone bad from his point of view and you cannot get round this. You can only wait, being ready for a gradual return of feeding.

Or the baby may start to wake screaming. You just help on the waking-up process. Or things may go well, but nevertheless you notice a change towards sadness in the child, a new note in the crying, perhaps going over into a musical note. This sadness is not necessarily bad. Don't just think sad babies need to be jogged up and down till they smile. They have something to be sad about, and sadness comes to an end if you wait.

The baby is sad at times like the weaning-time because circumstances have made anger come and spoil something that was good. In the baby's dreams the breasts are no longer good, they have been hated, and so now they are felt to be bad, even dangerous. That is why there is a place for the wicked woman in the fairy stories who gives poisoned apples. For the newly-weaned infant it is the really good mother whose breasts have become bad, and so there has to be time allowed for recovery and readjustment. But an ordinary good mother does not shirk even this. Often in the twenty-four hours she has to be the bad mother for a few minutes, and she gets used to this. In time she is seen as the good mother again. Eventually the child grows up and gets to know her just as she really is, neither ideal nor indeed a witch.

So, there is a wider aspect of weaning – weaning is not only getting a baby to take other foods, or to use a cup, or to feed actively using the hands. It includes the gradual process of disillusionment, which is part of the parents' task.

The ordinary good mother and father do not want to be worshipped by their children. They endure the extremes of being idealized and hated, hoping that eventually their children will see them as the ordinary human beings they certainly are.

Chapter 13

Further Thoughts on Babies as Persons

The human being's development is a continuous process. As in the development of the body, so in the development of the personality and in the development of the capacity for relationships. No stage can be missed or marred without ill-effect.

Health is maturity, maturity appropriate to the age. If certain accidental diseases are ignored this is obviously true of the body, and in matters of psychology there are practically no reasons why health and maturity should not mean the same thing. In other words, in the emotional development of a human being, if there are no hitches or distortions in the developmental process, there is health.

This means, if I am right, that all the care that a mother and father take of their infant is not just a pleasure to them and to the infant, it is also absolutely necessary, and without it the baby cannot easily grow up into a healthy or valuable adult.

In matters of the body it is possible to make mistakes, even to allow rickets, and yet rear a child with nothing worse than bow-legs. But on the psychological side, a baby deprived of some quite ordinary but necessary thing, such as affectionate contact, is bound, to some extent, to be disturbed in emotional development, and this will show in a personal difficulty as the young person grows up. Put the other way round; as a child grows and passes from stage to stage of complex internal development and eventually achieves a capacity for relationships, the parents can know that their good care has been an essential ingredient. This has a meaning for us all, for it follows that, in so far as we are reasonably mature or healthy as adults, each one of us must recognize that a good start to one's life was provided by someone. It is this good start – this basis for child care – that I try to describe.

The story of a human being does not start at five years or two, or at six months, but starts at birth – and before birth if you like; and each baby is from the start a person, and needs to be known by someone. No one can get to know a baby as well as the baby's own mother can.

These two statements take us a long way, but now, how to proceed? Can psychology tell anyone how to be a mother or father? I think this is the wrong way round. Let us, instead, study some of the things mothers and fathers naturally do, and try to show them a little why they do them, so that they may feel strengthened.

I will take an example.

Here is a mother with her baby girl. What does she do when she picks her up? Does she catch hold of her foot and drag her out of her pram and swing her up? Does she hold a cigarette with one hand and grab her with the other? No. She has quite a different way of going at it. I think she tends to give the infant warning of her approach, she puts her hands round her to gather her together before she moves her; in fact she gains the baby's cooperation before she lifts her; and then she lifts her from one place to another, from cot to shoulder. Does she not then put the baby up against her with her head snuggled in her neck, so that the baby may begin to feel her as a person?

Here is a mother with her baby boy. How does she bath him? Does she just put him in the electric washer and let the cleaning process happen mechanically? Not at all. She knows of bath-time as a special time both for her and for the baby. She prepares to enjoy it. She does all the mechanical part properly, testing the heat of the water with her elbow and not letting the baby slip through her fingers when he is soapy, but on top of this she allows the bathing to be an enjoyed experience which enriches the growing relationship, not only of herself to the baby, but of him to her.

Why does she take all this trouble? Can we not say quite simply, and without being sentimental, that it is because of love; that it is because maternal feelings have developed in her; because of the deep understanding of her baby's needs that comes from her devotion?

Let us go back to the business of picking a baby up. Can we not say that, without conscious effort, the mother did what she did in stages. She made being picked up acceptable to her little girl by:

(1) giving the infant warning;
(2) gaining her cooperation;
(3) gathering her together;
(4) taking her from one place to another and with a simple purpose that she can understand.

The mother also refrains from shocking her baby with cold hands, or from pricking him or her when she pins up the napkin.

The mother does not involve her baby in all her personal experiences and feelings. Sometimes her baby yells and yells until she feels like murder, yet she lifts the baby up with just the same care, without revenge – or not very much. She avoids making the baby the victim of her own impulsiveness. Infant care, like doctoring, is a test of personal reliability.

Today may be one of those days when everything goes wrong. The laundryman calls before the list is ready; the front-door bell rings, and someone else comes to the back door. But a mother waits till she has recovered her poise before she takes up her baby, which she does with the usual gentle technique that the baby comes to know as an important part of her. Her technique is highly personal, and is looked for and recognized, like her mouth, and her eyes, her colouring, and her smell. Over and over again a mother deals with her own moods, anxieties, and excitements in her own private life, reserving for her baby what belongs to the baby. This gives a foundation on which the human infant can start to build an understanding of the extremely complex thing that is a relationship between two human beings.

Can we not say that the mother *adapts herself* to what the baby can understand, actively adapts to needs? This active adaptation is just what is essential for the infant's emotional growth, and the mother adapts herself to the baby's needs especially at the beginning, at a time when only the simplest possible circumstances can be appreciated.

I must try to explain a little why it is that a mother takes all this trouble, and so much more than I can include in this brief description. One reason why I must do this is that there are some who honestly believe and who teach that in the first six months the mother does not matter. In the first six months (it is said) only technique counts, and a good technique can be provided in a hospital or a home, by trained workers.

For my part I am sure that while mothercraft may be taught and even read about in books, *the mothering of one's own baby is entirely personal, a job that no one else could take over and do as well as oneself.* While the scientists are at the problem, seeking proofs as they must do before believing, mothers will do well to insist that they themselves are needed from the start. This opinion, I may as well add, is not based on hearing mothers talk, on guess-work, or on pure intuition; it is the conclusion I feel I have been forced to draw after long research.

The mother takes trouble because she feels (and I find she is correct in this feeling), that if the human baby is to develop well and to develop richly there should be personal mothering from the start, if possible by the very person who has conceived and carried that baby, the one who has a very deeply rooted interest in allowing for that baby's point of view, and who loves to let herself be the baby's whole world.

This does not mean that a baby of a few weeks knows the mother as at six months or a year. In the very first days it is the pattern and technique of mothering that is perceived, and so also the detail of her nipples, the shape of her ear, the quality of her smile, the warmth and smell of her breath. Quite early an infant may have a rudimentary idea of a kind of wholeness of the mother at certain special moments. Apart from what can be perceived, however, the infant needs the mother to be continuously there as a whole person, for only as a whole and mature human being can she have the love and character required for the task.

I once risked the remark, 'There is no such thing as a baby' – meaning that if you set out to describe a baby, you will find you are describing a *baby and someone*. A baby cannot exist alone, but is essentially part of a relationship.

The mother, too, has to be considered. If the continuity of her relationship to her own baby is broken something is lost that cannot be regained. It shows incredible lack of understanding of the mother's role to take away her baby for a few weeks, then to hand the baby back, and expect the mother to continue just where she left off.

I will try to classify some ways in which a mother is needed.

(a) First I want to say that the mother is needed as a live person. Her baby must be able to feel the warmth of her skin and breath, and to taste and see. This is vitally important. There must be full access to the mother's live body. Without the mother's live presence the most learned mothercraft is wasted. It is the same with doctors. The value of a general practitioner in a village is largely that he is alive, that he is there and available. People know the number of his car, and the back view of his hat. It takes years to learn to be a doctor, the training may absorb all of a father's capital; but in the end the really important thing is not the doctor's learning and skill, but the fact that the village knows and feels that he is alive and available. The doctor's physical presence meets an emotional need. As with doctor so with mother, only much more so.

Psychology and physical care join here. During the war I was with a group of people who were discussing the future of the war-stricken children of Europe. They asked me for my opinion as to the most important *psychological* things to be done for these children at the end of the war. I found myself saying, 'Give them food.' Someone said, 'We don't mean physical things, we mean psychological things.' I still felt that the giving of food at the right moment would be catering for psychological need. Fundamentally, love expresses itself in physical terms.

Of course if physical care means having a baby vaccinated this has nothing to do with psychology. A baby cannot appreciate your concern lest smallpox should become rampant in the community – though the doctor's attack on his skin may of course produce crying. But if physical care means the right kind of meal at the right temperature at the right time (right from the baby's point of view, I mean), then this is psychological care too. I think this is a useful rule. The care that a baby can appreciate is fulfilling psychological and emotional needs, however much it may seem to be related simply to physical needs.

In this first way of looking at things the mother's aliveness and physical management provide an essential psychological and emotional milieu, essential for the baby's early emotional growth.

(b) Secondly, the mother is needed to present the world to the baby. Through the techniques of the person or the techniques of the people who are doing the minding comes the baby's introduction to external reality, to the world around. There will continue a struggle with this difficult matter all through life, but help is needed here especially at the start. I will explain what I mean with some care, because many mothers may never have thought of infant feeding in this way; certainly doctors and nurses seldom seem to consider this aspect of the feeding act. This is what I mean.

Imagine a baby who has never had a feed. Hunger turns up, and the baby is ready to conceive of something; out of need the baby is ready to create a source of satisfaction, but there is no previous experience to show the baby what there is to expect. If at this moment the mother places her breast where the baby is ready to expect something, and if plenty of time is allowed for the infant to feel round, with mouth and hands, and perhaps with a sense of smell, the baby 'creates' just what is there to be found. The baby eventually gets the illusion that this real breast is exactly the thing that was created out of need, greed, and the first impulses of primitive loving. Sight, smell, and taste register somewhere, and after a while the baby may be creating something like the very breast that mother has to offer. A thousand times before weaning a baby may be given just this particular introduction to external reality by one woman, the mother. A thousand times the feeling has existed that what was wanted was created, and was found to be there. From this develops a belief that the world can contain what is wanted and needed, with the result that the baby has hope that there is a live relationship between inner reality and external reality, between innate primary creativity and the world at large which is shared by all.

Successful infant feeding, therefore, is an essential part of the infant's education. In the same way, but I will not try to develop the theme here, the infant needs the mother's way of receiving the excretions. The infant needs the mother's acceptance of a relationship expressed in excretion terms, a relationship that is in full swing long before the infant can contribute by conscious effort, and before the infant can (perhaps at three, four, or six months) start to wish to give to the mother out of a sense of guilt; that is to say, to make reparation for greedy attack.

(c) Out of all that could be said I will add a third way in which the mother is needed, the mother herself, and not a team of excellent minders. I refer to the mother's job of *disillusioning*. When she has given her baby the illusion that the world can be created out of need and imagination (which of course in one sense it cannot be, but we can leave this to the philosopher), when she has established the belief in things and people that I have described as a healthy basis for development, she will then have to take the child through the process of disillusionment, which is a wider aspect of weaning. The nearest that can be offered to the child is the grown-ups' *wish* to make the demands of reality bearable until the full blast of disillusionment can be borne, and until creativity can develop through mature skill into a true contribution to society.

The 'shades of the prison house' seems to me to be the poet's description of the disillusioning process, and its essential painfulness. Gradually the mother enables the child to allow that though the world *can* provide something like what is needed and wanted, and what could therefore be created, it will not do so automatically, nor at the very moment the mood arises or the wish is felt.

Do you notice how I am gradually switching from the idea of need to that of a wish or desire? The change indicates a growing up, and an acceptance of external reality with a consequent weakening of instinctual imperative.

Temporarily the mother has put herself out for the child, she has at the beginning put herself in the child's pocket. But, eventually, this child becomes able to leave the dependence that belongs to the earliest stage when the environment must adapt itself, and can accept two coexisting points of view – the mother's as well as the baby's. But the mother cannot deprive the child of herself (weaning, disillusionment) unless she has first meant everything to the child.

It is not my intention to say that the baby's whole life is wrecked if there has been a failure actually at the *breast*. Of course a baby can thrive physically on the bottle given with reasonable skill, and a mother whose breast milk fails can do almost all that is needed in the course of bottle-feeding. Nevertheless, the principle holds that a baby's emotional development at the start is only to be built well on a relationship with one person, who should, ideally, be the mother. Who else will both feel and supply what is needed?

Chapter 14

The Innate Morality of the Baby

Sooner or later the question must be asked: how far should parents try to impose their standards and beliefs on the growing child? The ordinary thing would be to say that we are concerned here with 'training'. The word 'training' certainly brings to mind the sort of thing that I want to go into now, which is the business of how to get your baby to become nice and clean and good and obedient, sociable, moral, and so on. I was going to say happy too, but you cannot teach a child to be happy.

This word 'training' always seems to me to be something that belongs to the care of dogs. Dogs do need to be trained. I suppose we can learn something from dogs, in that if you know your own mind your dog is happier than if you do not; and children, too, like you to have your own ideas about things. But a dog doesn't have to grow up eventually into a human being, so when we come to your baby we have to start again, and the best thing is to see how far we can leave out the word 'training' altogether.

There's room for the idea that the sense of good and bad, like much else, comes naturally to each infant and child provided certain conditions of environmental care can be taken for granted. But it is a complex matter, this process of development from impulsiveness and claiming to control everyone and everything, to an ability to conform. I cannot tell you how complex it is. Such development takes time. Only if you feel it is worth while will you allow opportunity for what has to happen.

I am still talking about infants, but it is so very difficult to describe what is happening in the first months in infant terms. To make it easier, let us look now at a boy of five or six drawing. I shall pretend he is conscious of what is going on, though he is not really. He is making a picture. What does he do? He knows the impulse to scribble and to make a mess. That is not a picture. These primitive pleasures have to be kept fresh, but at the same time he wants to express ideas, and also to express them in such a way that they may possibly be understood. If he achieves a picture he has found a series of controls that satisfies him. First of all there is a piece of paper of a particular size and shape which he accepts. Then he hopes to use a certain amount of skill that has come of practice. Then he knows that the picture when it is finished must have balance – you know, the tree on either side of the house – this is an expression of the fairness which he needs and probably gets from the parents. The points of interest must balance, and so must the lights and shades and the colour scheme. The interest of the picture must be spread over the whole paper, and yet there must be a central theme which knits the whole thing together. Within this system of accepted, indeed self-imposed, controls he tries to express an idea, and to keep some of the freshness of feeling that belonged to the idea when it was born. It almost takes my breath away to describe all this, yet your children achieve it quite naturally if you will give them half a chance.

Of course, as I said, he does not know all those things in a way that would make it possible for him to talk about them. Still less does an infant know what is going on within.

The baby is rather like this older boy, only at first it is much more obscure. The pictures don't actually get painted, in fact of course they are not pictures at all, but they are little contributions to society which only the mother of the baby is sensitive enough to appreciate. A smile can contain all this, or a clumsy gesture of the arm, or a sucking noise indicating readiness for a feed. Perhaps there is a whimpering sound by which the sensitive mother knows that if she comes quickly she may be able to attend personally to a motion which otherwise becomes just a wasted mess. This is the very beginning of cooperation and social sense, and is worth all the trouble it involves. How many children who wet the bed for some years after they could get up, and save a lot of washing, are going back in the night to their infancy, trying to go over their experience again, trying to find and correct something that was missing. The thing missing in that case was the mother's sensitive attention to signals of excitement or distress which would have enabled her to make personal and good what otherwise had to be wasted, because there was no one there to participate in what happened.

Just as the baby needs to link his physical experiences to a loving relationship with the mother, so he needs this relationship as a framework for his fears. These fears are primitive in nature, and are based on the infant's expectation of crude retaliations. The infant gets excited, with aggressive or destructive impulses or ideas, which he shows as screaming or wanting to bite, and immediately the world seems to be full of biting mouths and hostile teeth and claws and all kinds of threats. In this way the infant's world would be a terrifying place were it not for the mother's general protective role which hides these very great fears that belong to the infant's early experience of living. The mother (and I'm not forgetting the father) alters the quality of the small child's fears by being a human being. Gradually the mother, and others, are recognized by the infant as human beings. So instead of a world of magical retaliations, the infant acquires a parent who understands, and who reacts to the infant's impulses, and who can be hurt or made angry. When I put it this way you will see immediately that it makes an immense difference to the infant whether the retaliatory forces become humanized or not. For one thing, the mother knows the difference between actual destruction and the intention to destroy. She says 'Ow!' when she gets bitten. But she is not disturbed at all by recognizing that the baby wants to eat her. In fact, she feels that this is a compliment, and the way the baby shows excited love. And of course, she is not too easy to eat. She says 'Ow!' but that only means that she felt some pain. A baby can hurt the breast, especially if teeth unfortunately appear early. But mothers do survive, and babies have a chance to gain reassurance from the survival of the object. You give babies something hard, something which has good survival value, like a rattle or a bone ring, because you know that it is a relief for the baby to be able to bite all out.

In these early stages what is adaptive or 'good' in the environment is building up in the infant's storehouse of experiences as a self quality, indistinguishable at first from the infant's own healthy functioning. And while the baby is consciously aware of each failure of reliability, the storing of the 'good' experiences is a process that is not a matter of consciousness.

There are two ways in which a child can be introduced to standards of cleanliness and morality, and later to religious and political beliefs. One is for the parents to implant such standards and beliefs, to force the baby or the child into accepting them, making no attempt to integrate them with the developing personality. Sadly, there are children whose development is so unsatisfactory that this is the only way for them.

The second way is to allow and encourage the innate tendencies towards morality. Because of the mother's sensitive ways, which belong to the fact of her love, the roots of the infant's personal moral sense are preserved. We have seen how the baby hates to waste an experience, and much prefers to wait, and bear frustration of primitive pleasures, if waiting adds the warmth of a personal relationship. And we have seen how the mother helps to provide the framework of a loving relationship for the infant's feelings of activity and violence. In the process of integration, impulses to attack and destroy, and impulses to give and share are related, one lessening the effect of the other. Coercive training fails to make use of this child's integrative process.

What I am describing here is in fact the gradual build-up in the child of a capacity to feel a sense of responsibility, which at base is a sense of guilt. The environmental essential here is the continued presence of the mother or mother-figure over the period of time in which the child is accommodating the destructiveness that is part of his or her make-up. This destructiveness becomes more and more a feature in the experience of object relationships, and the phase of development to which I am referring lasts from about six months to two years after which the child may have made a satisfactory fusion of the idea of destroying the object with the fact of loving the same object. The mother is needed over this time and she is needed because of her survival value. She is an environment mother and at the same time an object mother, the object of excited loving. The child gradually comes to integrate these two

aspects of the mother and to be able to love and to be affectionate with the mother at the same time. This involves the
child in a special kind of anxiety which is called a sense of
guilt. The infant gradually becomes able to tolerate feeling
anxious (guilty) about the destructive elements in instinctual
experiences, because he knows that there will be opportunity
for repairing and rebuilding.

The balance implied here gives a deeper sense of right and
wrong than any merely imposed parental standards. What it
does owe to the mother is the reliable environment provided
by her love. We can see the capacity for a sense of guilt disap-
pearing, along with the loss of confidence in the reliability
of the environment, as when a mother has to be away from
her infant, or when she is ill, or perhaps preoccupied.

We can if we like think of the child as developing an internal
good mother, who feels it is a happy achievement to get any
experience within the orbit of a human relationship. When
this has begun to happen, the mother's own sensitivity can
become less intense. At the same time she can begin to rein-
force and enrich the child's developing morality.

Civilization has started again inside a new human being, and
the parents should have some moral code waiting for their
child when, much later, he starts looking for one. One function
of this will be to humanize the child's own cripplingly fierce
morality, his hatred of compliance at the expense of a personal
way of life. It is good for this fierce morality to be humanized,
but it must not be killed – as it can be by parents understand-
ably putting too great a value on peace and quiet. Compliance
brings immediate rewards and adults only too easily mistake
compliance for growth.

Chapter 15

Instincts and Normal Difficulties

When it comes to illness, talks and books are rather misleading. What a mother needs for her ill child is a doctor who can see and examine the baby and have a discussion with her. But the common troubles of ordinary healthy children are a different matter, and I think mothers find it rather helpful when it is pointed out to them that their well children are not to be expected to go straight ahead without giving any cause for worry and anxiety.

Ordinary healthy children undoubtedly do present all kinds of symptoms.

What is it that causes these troubles in infancy and early childhood? If we take it for granted that your management has been skilled and consistent, so that you can be said to have laid down the foundations for the health of this new member of society satisfactorily, what is it that determines that the child still presents problems? The answer is, I think, chiefly to do with the matter of instincts. It is about this that I wish to write now.

It may be that just for the moment your child is lying quietly over there sleeping, or cuddling something, or playing, in one of those quiet periods that you welcome. But you know only too well that in health there are recurring excitements. You can either look at it one way and say that the child gets hungry, that the body has needs, or instincts, or else you look at it another way, and say that the child begins to have exciting ideas. These exciting experiences play a very important part in the child's development, promoting as well as complicating growth.

During excitement the child has impelling needs. Often you are able to satisfy them. The needs, however, can be very great indeed, at certain moments, and some of them cannot be satisfied fully.

Now some of these needs (hunger for example) are universally recognized and easy to bring to your notice. The nature of other kinds of excitement is less widely understood.

The fact is that any part of the body may be excited at one time or another. The skin, for instance. You have seen children scratching their faces, or scratching the skin in other places, the skin itself becoming excited, and developing some kind of rash. And there are certain parts of the skin that are more sensitive than others, especially at certain times. You can go over the whole of the body of the child and think out the various ways in which excitement becomes localized. We certainly cannot leave out the sexual parts. These things are very important to the infant, and they make up the high lights of the waking life of infancy. Exciting ideas go along with the bodily excitements, and you will not be surprised if I say that these ideas not only have to do with pleasure, they also have to do with love, if the baby is developing well. Gradually the infant becomes a person capable of loving persons, and feeling loved as a person. There is a very powerful bond between the baby and the mother and father and other people around, and the excitements have to do with this love. In the form of some bodily excitement, love periodically becomes acutely felt.

The ideas that go with the primitive love impulses are predominantly destructive, and are nearly related to those of anger. The result for the baby feels good, however, if the activity leads to instinctual gratifications.

You can easily see that during such periods there is inevitably a great deal of frustration, and this leads in health to anger, even rage. You will not think your infant is ill if from time to time you are presented with a picture of rage, which you learn to distinguish from sadness, fear, and pain. In rage the infant's heart is beating faster than it will ever beat again. In fact, as many as 220 heart beats a minute can be counted, if you want to listen. Anger means that the child has got as far as believing in something and in someone to be angry with.

Now, a risk is taken whenever emotions are fully felt, and these experiences of excitement and rage must often be very painful; so you will find your perfectly normal child trying to discover ways of avoiding the most intense feelings. One way of avoiding feelings is by a damping down of instinct – for instance, the infant becomes unable to let the full extent of the excitement of feeding take place. Another way is accepting certain kinds of food but not other kinds. Or other people may give the feed, but not the mother. Every possible variation can be found, if one knows enough children. This is not necessarily illness; it is simply that we see little children discovering all sorts of techniques for managing feelings which are intolerable. They have to avoid a certain amount of natural feelings because these are too intense, or else because the full experience brings about painful conflicts.

Feeding difficulties are common in normal children, and it often happens that mothers have to put up with very disappointing months, and even years, in which a child wastes all their ability to provide good food. Perhaps a child only takes routine food, and anything prepared with special care or delicacy is rejected. Sometimes mothers have to let children refuse food altogether for quite a long time, for if they try to force it in such circumstances they only increase the child's resistance. If they wait, however, and do not make a 'thing' out of it, at some time or other the child will start eating again. One can well imagine a mother who is not experienced being worried during such a period, and needing a doctor or a nurse to reassure her that she is not neglecting her child, or doing harm.

Infants periodically have various kinds of orgy (not only feeding orgies), and these orgies are natural, and very important to them. Their excretory processes are particularly exciting to them, and the sexual parts of their bodies even more so, at appropriate moments, as they grow. It is of course easy to see the boy's erection, and difficult to know what the little girl baby feels sexually.

By the way, you will have noticed that babies do not start off thinking the same as you do about what is nice and what is nasty. Stuff that is got rid of with excitement and pleasure is likely to be felt to be good, and even good to eat, and good to smear the cot and the walls with. That may be a nuisance, but it is natural, and you will not mind too much. You will be contented to wait for more civilized sentiments to turn up of their own accord. Sooner or later disgust turns up, and, even quite suddenly, a baby who was eating soap and drinking bathwater will become prudish, and go off any kind of food that even looks like excretions, which were (till a few days previously) handled and pushed into the mouth.

Sometimes we see a return to the infant state in older children, and then we know that some difficulty has blocked the way to progress, and the child has a need to go back over the ground covered in infancy, in order to re-establish the rights of infants and the laws of natural development.

Mothers watch these things happening, and, as mothers, they do indeed play a part in it all; but they would rather watch a steady and natural developmental process than impose their own ideas of right and wrong.

One trouble that comes from trying to impose a pattern of right and wrong on an infant is that the infant's instincts come along and spoil it all. The moments of excited experience break down the baby's efforts to gain love through compliance. The result then is that he or she becomes upset, instead of strengthened, by the operation of the instincts.

The normal child has not too severely squashed the powerful instinctual feelings back, and is therefore subject to disturbances, and these look like symptoms to the ignorant observer. I have mentioned rage; temper tantrums and periods of absolute defiance are usual at two and three. Nightmares are frequently experienced by little children, and the piercing yells at midnight make the neighbours wonder what you are up to. But the truth is that the child has had a dream with some kind of sexuality in it.

Young children do not have to be ill to be frightened of dogs, doctors, and the dark, or to be imaginative about sounds and shadows, and vague shapes in the twilight; and they do not have to be ill to be liable to colic, or to sickness, or to going green when they are excited about something; they do not have to be ill to refuse to have anything to do with an adored father for a week or two, or to refuse to say 'ta' to an aunt; and they do not have to be ill to want to put the new sister in the dustbin, or to be rather cruel to the cat in a big effort to avoid hating the new baby.

And you know all about the way clean children become dirty, and dry ones wet, and how, in fact, in the period from two to five almost anything can happen. Put it all down to the workings of the instincts, and to the terrific feelings that belong to the instincts, and (since with all bodily happenings there are ideas) to the painful conflicts that result from all this in the child's imagination. Let me add that at this critical age the instincts are no longer just infantile in quality, and in describing them we do not say enough if we keep to the nursery terms, such as 'greediness' and 'messing'. When a healthy three-year-old child says 'I love you' there is meaning in it like that between men and women who love, and who are in love. It can, in fact, be sexual in the ordinary sense, involving the bodily sex parts, and including ideas that are like those of adolescents or adults in love. Tremendous forces are at work, yet all you need to do is to keep the home together, and to expect anything. Relief will come through the operation of time. When the child is five or six, things will then sober down a lot, and will stay sobered down till puberty, so you will have an easier few years, during which you can hand part of the responsibility and part of the task over to the schools, and to the trained teachers.

Chapter 16

Young Children and Other People

The emotional development of an infant starts at the beginning of his life. If we are to judge the way in which a human being deals with his fellow creatures, and see how he builds up his personality and life, we cannot afford to leave out what happens in the earliest years, months, and even weeks and days of his life. When we approach the problems of adults, for instance those associated with marriage, we are, of course, confronted with a great deal that belongs to later development. Nevertheless, in the study of any one individual we find the past as well as the present, the infant as well as the adult. Feelings and thoughts which can conveniently be called sexual appear at an early age, much earlier than was allowed for in the philosophy of our grandparents, and in a sense the whole range of human relationships is there from the start.

Let us see what happens when healthy small children play at fathers and mothers. On the one hand we can be sure that sex comes into the game, although very often not by direct representation. It is possible to detect many symbols of adult sex behaviour, but it is not with this that I am concerned at the present moment. More important from our point of view is that these children are enjoying in their play something which is based on their ability to feel identified with their parents. Obviously they have observed a great deal. One can see in their games that they are building a home, arranging the house, taking joint responsibility for the children, even maintaining a framework in which the children in this game can discover their own spontaneity. (For children become frightened of their own impulses if left entirely on their own.) We know this is healthy; if children can play together like this they will not need later on to be taught how to build a home. They know the essentials already. Putting it the other way round, is it possible to teach people how to build a home if they have never had it in them to play fathers and mothers? I should think probably not.

While we are glad to see children thus able to enjoy games which show their ability to become identified with the home and with the parents, and with a mature outlook and a sense of responsibility, these are not things that we want our children to achieve all day long. Indeed, it would be alarming if they did so. We expect the same children who play this game in the afternoon to be just greedy children at tea-time, jealous of each other at bed-time, naughty and defiant the next morning; for they are still children. If they are lucky their real home exists. In the setting of their real home, they can go on discovering their own spontaneity and individuality, letting themselves go, as a story-teller does, surprising himself at the ideas that turn up as he warms to his task. In real life they can use their own real parents, although in the game they seek in turns to be the parents themselves. We welcome the appearance of this game of home-building along with all the other games of teachers and pupils, doctors, nurses, and patients, bus drivers and passengers.

We can see the health in it all. But by the time children have reached this stage at which they play games, we can easily understand that they have already been through many complex processes of development, and these processes are, of course, not ever actually completed. If children need an ordinary good home with which to become identified, they also deeply need a stable home and a stable emotional environment in which they can have the opportunity to make steady and natural progress, in their own time, through the very early stages of development. By the way, it is not necessary for parents to know all that goes on in the minds of their small children, any more than they need know all about anatomy and physiology in order to give their children physical health. It is essential for them, however, to have the imagination to recognize that parental love is not merely a natural instinct within themselves, but it is something which a child absolutely needs of them.

The baby is in a bad way who is cared for by a mother who, though well-meaning, believes that babies are little more at the beginning than a bundle of physiology and anatomy and conditioned reflexes. No doubt the baby will be well fed, and he may achieve physical health and growth, but unless his mother can see the human being in the new-born infant, there is but little chance that mental health will be soundly based in such a way that the child in later life can have a rich stable personality that can not only adapt to the world, but also be part of the world which demands adaptation.

The trouble is that the mother naturally tends to be afraid of her great responsibility, and she easily flies to the textbooks and the rules and regulations. The proper care of an infant can only be done from the heart; perhaps I should say that the head cannot do it alone, but can do it only if feelings are free.

Giving food is only one of the ways in which a mother makes herself known to her infant, but it is an important one. I wrote earlier that the child who has been sensitively fed at the beginning and sensitively managed in other ways has really got beyond any answer that can be given to our philosophical conundrum, 'Is that object over there really there, or is it only imagined?' Whether the object is real or illusory has become relatively unimportant to him because he has found a mother who has been willing *to provide him with the illusion*, and to provide it unfailingly and for a long enough period so that the gulf that there can be between what can be imagined and what is actually to be found has been reduced for this child personally as much as it is possible for it to be reduced.

Such a child has established at the end of his nine or so months a good relationship to something outside himself which he is coming to recognize as his mother, a relationship which is able to survive all possible frustrations and complications and even loss by separation. The baby who has been fed mechanically and insensitively and with no one wanting actively to adapt to the needs of that particular infant is at a great disadvantage, and if such a baby can conceive of a devoted mother at all such a mother must remain an imaginary idealized figure.

We may easily find a mother who is unable to live in the world of the infant, who must live in the mother's world.

Such a child may make very good progress from the point of view of the superficial observer. It may not be until adolescence or even later that he at last makes appropriate protest, and either breaks down or finds mental health only in defiance.

In contrast, the mother who actively adapts in a rich way gives her baby a basis for making contact with the world, and more than that, gives a richness to the baby's relationship with the world which can develop and come to fruition as maturity follows in the course of time. A not unimportant part of this initial relationship of the baby with the mother is the inclusion in it of powerful instinctual drives; the survival of the baby and the mother teaches the baby through experience that instinctual experiences and excited ideas can be allowed, and that they do not necessarily destroy the quiet type of relationship, friendship, and sharing.

It should not be concluded that every baby who is sensitively fed and managed by a devoted mother is necessarily bound to develop complete mental health. Even when the early experiences are good, everything gained has to be consolidated in the course of time. Nor should it be concluded that every baby who is brought up in an institution, or by a mother who is unimaginative or too frightened to trust her own judgement, is destined for the mental hospital or Borstal. Things are not so simple as this. I have deliberately simplified the problem for the sake of clarity.

We have already seen that the healthy little child who is born into good conditions, whose mother has treated him as a person in his own right from the start, is not just nice, and good, and compliant. The normal child has a personal view of life from the beginning. Healthy babies often have quite strong feeding difficulties; they may be defiant and wilful in regard to their excretions; they protest often and vehemently with screaming, they kick their mothers and pull their mothers' hair, and they try to gouge their eyes out; in fact they are a nuisance. But they display spontaneous and absolutely genuine affectionate impulses, a hug here and a little bit of generosity there; through these things the mother's of such infants find reward.

Somehow the textbooks seem to like good, compliant, clean children, but these virtues are only of value when the children develop them in the course of time, because of their growing ability to become identified with the parental side of home life. This is rather like the natural progression in a child's artistic efforts, which was described in an earlier chapter.

Nowadays we so often speak of the maladjusted child, but the maladjusted child is one to whom the *world* has failed to adjust adequately at the beginning and in the early stages. The compliance of an infant is a terrible thing. It means that the parents are buying convenience at a heavy price, which will have to be paid over and over again either by them, or by society if the parents cannot stand the racket.

I should like to mention a difficulty in this matter of the earliest relationship between the mother and the infant which concerns any prospective mother. At the time of the birth of the baby and for the few days afterwards, the doctor must be an important person for her, the one who is responsible for what goes on, and in whom she has confidence. There is nothing more important at such a time than for the mother to know her doctor, and the nurse who works with the doctor. Unfortunately it cannot be assumed that the doctor who is so very skilled in regard to physical health and physical disease and with the whole problem of the management of child-birth is equally well informed in regard to the emotional tie between the baby and the mother. There is so much for a doctor to learn that he can hardly be expected to be an expert on the physical side and also to be right up to date with the latest that there is to be known about the psychology of mothers and their babies. It is always possible, therefore, that an excellent doctor or nurse may interfere, without meaning to do any harm at all, in this delicate matter of the first contact between mother and baby.

The mother indeed does need the doctor and the nurse, and their skill, and the framework which they provide enables her to put her worries aside. Within that framework, however, she needs to be able to find her infant and to enable her infant to find her. She needs to be able to let this happen in a natural way, not according to any rules that can be found in books.

Mothers need not feel ashamed to find they are specialists just at this point where the doctor and the nurse are only in a position to assist.

There can be observed a general cultural tendency away from direct contact, away from the clinical, away from what used to be called vulgar, that is to say naked, natural, and real, and there is a tendency towards whatever is at one remove from actual physical contact and interchange.

There is another way in which the infant's emotional life forms the basis for the emotional life of the individual at a later stage. I have spoken about the way in which instinctual drives enter the relationship of the infant to the mother right from the beginning. Along with these powerful instincts are the aggressive elements, and also there is all the hate and anger that arise from frustration. The aggressive element in, and associated with, the excited love impulses makes life feel very dangerous, and because of this most individuals become to some extent inhibited. It is perhaps profitable to look at this part of the problem a little more closely.

I would say that the most primitive and early impulses are felt ruthlessly. If there is a destructive element in the early feeding impulse the infant is at first not concerned with the consequences. I am, of course, talking about the ideas, and not just about the actual physical processes which we can watch with our eyes. At first the infant is carried away by impulses, and only very gradually there comes the realization that the thing attacked in an excited feeding experience is a vulnerable part of the mother, the other human being who is so much valued as a person in the quiet intervals between excitements and orgies. The excited infant violently attacks the mother's body in fantasy although the attack that we see is but feeble; satisfaction comes with the feeding experience, and for the time being the attack ceases. Every physical process is enriched by fantasy, which steadily develops definiteness and complexity as the baby grows. In the baby's fantasy the mother's body was torn open so that the good things could be got at and incorporated. How important it is, therefore, for a baby to have his mother consistently looking after him, looking after him over a period of time, surviving his attacks, and eventually there to be the object of the tender feeling and the guilt feeling and sense of concern for her welfare which come along in the course of time. Her continuing to be a live person in the baby's life makes it possible for the baby to find that innate sense of guilt which is the only valuable guilt feeling, and which is the main source of the urge to mend and to re-create and to give. There is a natural sequence of ruthless love, aggressive attack, guilt feeling, sense of concern, sadness, desire to mend and build and give; this sequence is the essential experience of infancy and early childhood and yet it cannot become a real thing unless the mother, or someone doing her job for her, is able to live through the phases with the infant, and so to make possible the integration of the various elements.

And here is yet another way of stating some of the things that the ordinary good mother is doing for her infant. Without undue difficulty and without knowing what she is doing, the average good parent is all the time helping the child to distinguish between the actual happenings and what goes on in the imagination. She is sorting out for the infant the actual from the enriching fantasy. We say she is being objective. In the matter of aggression this is particularly important. A mother protects herself from being bitten badly and she prevents the two-year-old child from hitting the new baby on the head with a poker, but at the same time she recognizes the tremendous force and reality of the destructive and aggressive *ideas* that belong to the child who is behaving tolerably well, and she is not alarmed by ideas. She knows that ideas must be there, and when they gradually appear in play or in dreams she is not surprised, and she even provides stories and story-books which carry on the themes that arise spontaneously in the child mind. She does not try to prevent the child from having ideas of destruction, and in that way she enables innate guilt to develop in its own way. It is innate guilt that we hope will turn up as the infant develops, and for which we are willing to wait; imposed morality bores us.

The period in which one is called on to be a mother or father is certainly a time of self-sacrifice. The ordinary good mother knows without being told that during this time nothing must interfere with the continuity of the relationship between the child and herself. Does she know that when she is acting quite naturally in this way, not only is she laying the foundation of the mental health of her child, but also the child cannot achieve mental health without having at the beginning just that experience which she is taking so much trouble to provide?

Part Two

The Family

Chapter 17

What About Father?

In my job many mothers have discussed with me the question: What about father? I suppose it is clear to everyone that, in normal times, it depends on what mother does about it whether father does or does not get to know his baby. There are all sorts of reasons why it is difficult for a father to take part in his infant's upbringing. For one thing he may scarcely ever be at home when the baby is awake. But very often, even when father is home, mother finds it a little difficult to know when to make use of her husband, and when to wish him out of the way. No doubt it is often far simpler to get the baby to bed before father comes home, just as it is a good idea to get the washing done and the food cooked. But many of you will agree from your experience that it is a great help in the relation between married people when they share day by day the little details of experience in the care of their infant, little details which seem silly to outsiders, but which are tremendously important at the time, both to the parents and to the infant. And as the infant grows into a toddler and into a little child, the richness of detail increases and with this the bond between father and mother can become even deeper.

I know that some fathers are very shy about their babies at the beginning, and no doubt some can never be brought to be interested in infants; but, at any rate, mothers can get their husbands to help in little things, and can arrange for the baby to be bathed when father can watch, and even take part if he wants to. As I have said, it depends quite a lot on what you do about it.

One could not assume in every case that it is a good thing for father to come early into the picture. People are so different from each other. Some men feel as if they would be better mothers than their wives are, and they can be quite a nuisance. This is specially true when they are able to waltz in and be very patient 'mothers' for about half an hour, and then waltz out again, ignoring the fact that mothers have to be good mothers twenty-four hours a day, day in and day out. And then it may be that there are some fathers who really would make better mothers than their wives, but still they cannot be mothers; so some way out of the difficulty has to be found, other than by just letting mother fade out of the picture. But usually mothers know they are good at their own job, and then they can let their husbands into the picture if they wish.

If we start at the beginning we can see that the infant first of all knows mother. Sooner or later certain qualities of mother are recognized by the infant, and some of these – softness, sweetness – one associates always with a mother. But mother has all sorts of stern qualities as well: for instance, she can be hard, severe, and strict; indeed, her punctuality about feeds is valued tremendously by the infant as soon as he can accept the fact that he cannot be fed just exactly when he wants to feed. I would say that certain qualities of mother that are not essentially part of her gradually group together in the infant's mind, and these qualities draw to themselves the feelings which the infant at length becomes willing to have towards father. How much better a strong father who can be respected and loved than just a combination of qualities of mother, rules and regulations, permits and prohibitions, things dead and uncompromising.

So when father comes into the child's life as a father, he takes over feelings that the infant has already had towards certain properties of mother, and it is a great relief to mother when father can take over in this way.

Let me see if I can separate out the different ways in which father is valuable. The first thing I want to say is that father is needed at home to help mother to feel well in her body and happy in her mind. A child is very sensitive indeed to the re-lationship between the parents, and if all goes well off-stage, so to speak, the child is the first to appreciate the fact, and tends to show this appreciation by finding life easier, and by being more contented and more easy to manage. I suppose this is what an infant or a child would mean by 'social security'.

The sexual union of father and mother provides a fact, a

hard fact around which the child may build a fantasy, a rock to which he can cling and against which he can kick; and furthermore it provides part of the natural foundation for a personal solution to the problem of the triangular relationship.

The second thing, as I have said, is that father is needed to give mother moral support, to be the backing for her authority, to be the human being who stands for the law and order which mother plants in the life of the child. He does not have to be there all the time to do this, but he has to turn up often enough for the child to feel that he is real and alive. Much of the arranging of a child's life must be done by mother, and children like to feel that mother can manage the home when father is not actually in it. Indeed, every woman has to be able to speak and act with authority; but if she has to be the whole thing, and has to provide the whole of the strong or strict element in her children's lives as well as the love, she carries a big burden indeed. Besides, it is much easier for the children to be able to have two parents; one parent can be felt to remain loving while the other is being hated, and this in itself has a stabilizing influence. Sometimes you see a child hitting or kicking his mother, and you feel that if her husband were backing her up the child would probably want to kick him, and very likely would not try it on at all. Every now and again the child is going to hate someone, and if father is not there to tell him where to get off, he will hate his mother, and this will make him confused, because it is his mother that he loves most fundamentally.

The third thing to say is that father is needed by the child because of his positive qualities and the things that distinguish him from other men, and the liveliness of his personality. During the early period of life, when impressions are so vivid, then is the time for a little boy or girl to get to know father, if this is possible. Of course, I'm not asking fathers to force themselves and their personalities on their children. One child will look round for father when a few months old, reach out to him when he comes into the room, and listen for his footsteps, whereas another will turn away from him, or only very gradually allow him to become an important person in his or her life. One child will want to know what he is really like, whereas another will use father as someone to dream about, hardly getting to know him at all as others know him. Nevertheless, if father is there and wants to get to know his own child the child is fortunate, and in the happiest circumstances father vastly enriches his child's world. When both mother and father easily accept responsibility for the child's existence the stage is set for a good home.

It is hardly possible to begin to describe the ways in which a father enriches the life of his children, so wide are the possibilities. The children form their ideal, at least in part, on what they see, or think they see, when they look at him. They get a new world opened up to them when father gradually discloses the nature of the work to which he goes in the morning, and from which he returns at night.

In the children's play there is the game 'Mothers and Fathers' and, as you know, father goes off in the morning to work, while mother does the housework and minds the children. Housework is something that children easily get to know because it is always going on around them, but the work that father does, to say nothing of his hobbies when he is off duty, widens the children's view of the world. How happy the children of a skilled craftsman who, when he is at home, is not above letting the children see the skill of his hands, and share in the making of beautiful and useful things. And if father sometimes joins in their play, he is bound to bring valuable new elements that can be woven into the playing. Moreover, father's knowledge of the world enables him to see when certain kinds of toys or apparatus would help the children in their play without hindering the natural development of their imagination. Some fathers, unfortunately, spoil it when they buy their little boy a steam engine, by playing with it themselves, or else by being so fond of it that they cannot let the child use it and perhaps break it. This is carrying father's play too far.

One of the things that father does for his children is to be alive and to stay alive during the children's early years. The value of this simple act is liable to be forgotten. Although it is natural for children to idealize their fathers, it is also very valuable for them to have the experience of living with them and getting to know them as human beings, even to the extent of finding them out. I know of a boy and girl who thought they were having a lovely time in the last war when their father was in the army. They lived with their mother in a house with a nice garden, and had everything that was necessary, and even more. Sometimes they worked up into a state of organized anti-social activity and nearly broke the house up. Now, as they look back, they can see that these periodical outbursts were attempts, unconscious at the time, to make their father appear in person. However, their mother managed to see them through, supported by letters from her husband; but you can imagine how much she longed to have him home with her, so that she could occasionally sit back while he told the children to go to bed.

To take an extreme case: I knew a girl whose father died before she was born. The tragedy here was that she had only an idealized father on whom to base her view of man. She had not the experience of being let down gently by a real father. In her life she easily imagined men to be ideal, which at first had the effect of bringing out the best in them. But sooner or later, inevitably, each man she got to know showed imperfections, and each time this happened she was thrown into a state of despair, and was continually complaining. As you can imagine, this pattern ruined her life. How much happier she would have been if her father had been alive during her childhood, to be felt by her to be ideal, but also to be found by her to have shortcomings, and to have survived her hate of him when he disappointed her.

It is well known that there is sometimes an especially vital bond between a father and his daughter. As a matter of fact, every little girl has it in her to dream of being in mother's place, or at any rate to dream romantically. Mothers have to be very understanding when this sort of feeling is going on. Some mothers find it much easier to stand the friendship between father and son than between father and daughter. Yet it is a great pity if the close bond between father and daughter is interfered with by feelings of jealousy and rivalry instead of being allowed to develop naturally; for sooner or later the little girl will realize the frustration that belongs to this kind of romantic attachment, and she will eventually grow up and look in other directions for the practical outcome to her imaginings. If father and mother are happy in relation to each other, these strong attachments between a father and his children will not be thought of as rivalling the attachment between the parents. Brothers are a great help here, providing a stepping-stone from fathers and uncles to men in general.

It is also well known that a boy and his father do find themselves at times in a state of rivalry over mother. This need give rise to no anxiety if mother and father are happy together. It need never, of course, interfere with the relationship between two parents who feel secure in each other's love. The little boy's feelings are of the strongest possible order, so they should be taken seriously.

One hears of children who never once in the whole of their childhood had father alone to themselves for a whole day, or even half a day. This seems to me to be terrible. I should say that it is mother's responsibility to send father and daughter, or father and son, out together for an expedition every now and again. This gesture will always be fully appreciated by all concerned, and some of these experiences will be treasured throughout a lifetime. It is not always easy for a mother to send her little girl out with father when she would love to go out herself alone with him; and, of course, she should go out with father alone as well, or else she will not only build up resentment in herself, but she will also be liable to lose touch with her man. But sometimes, if she can send father out with the children, or with one of them, she will be adding a great deal to her value as a mother and wife.

So if your husband is home, you may easily find that it is worth taking a lot of trouble to help him and the children to get to know each other. It is not in your power to make their relationship a rich one; that depends on father and the children. But it is very much in your power to make such a relationship possible, or to prevent it, or to mar it.

Chapter 18

Their Standards and Yours

I suppose all people have ideals and standards. Everyone who is building a home has ideas about the way things should look, and about the colour scheme, and about the furniture, and the way the table is laid for breakfast. Most people know just what sort of a house they would have if their ship came in, and whether they feel it is good to live in town or country, and what sort of a film it is worth while going to see.

When you got married you felt – 'now I can live as I like'.

A little girl of five who was collecting words had heard someone say 'the dog went home of his own accord,' so she adopted the word. Next day she said to me, 'Today's my birthday, so everything has to be my accord.' Well, when you married you felt: 'now at last I can live in an atmosphere which is my own accord,' to use the language of the little girl. Mind you, it isn't that your accord is necessarily better than your mother-in-law's, but it is yours, and that makes all the difference.

Assuming that you got your own rooms or flat or house, you straightway proceeded to arrange and decorate in the way you felt like doing. And when you had put up the new curtains you asked people in to see your home. The point is that you had achieved a state of affairs in which you expressed yourself in your surroundings, and you may have surprised even yourself by the way you did things. Evidently you had been practising for this all your life.

You were lucky in those early days if you escaped some squabbles with your husband over details. The funny thing is that arguments nearly always start about whether this or that is 'good' or 'bad', whereas the real trouble is a clash of accords, as the little girl might have said. This carpet is good for you if you bought it, or chose it, or bargained for it at a sale, and it is good from your husband's point of view if he chose it; but how can you both feel you chose it? Fortunately people who are in love do often find it possible to let their 'accords' overlap to some extent, for a while, so that is all right for a bit; and one way out of the difficulty is for it to be agreed, perhaps without anything being actually said, that the wife runs the home her way while the man has his own way at work. Everyone knows that the Englishman's home is his wife's castle. And in his home a man likes to see his wife in charge, identified with the home. Alas, all too often the man has nothing in his work corresponding to his wife's independence in her own home. Too seldom does a man feel identified with his job, and this state of affairs has been getting worse as craftsmen, and small shopkeepers, and small men generally have been tending to become swamped out.

Talk about women not wanting to be housewives seems to me to ignore one thing, that nowhere else but in her own home is a woman in such command. Only in her own home is she free, if she has the courage, to spread herself, to find her whole self. The great thing is that she should really be able to get a flat or a house when she marries, so that she can move her elbows without brushing up against her near relations, and without bruising her own mother.

I have said all this because I want to show how difficult it must always be when a baby comes along wanting his own way, as babies do. By wanting his own way the baby is upsetting the apple-cart, and no one should say it does not matter if it does get upset. The apple-cart is the young mother's newly-found independence of spirit and newly-won respect for what she does of her own accord. Some women prefer to have no children, because marriage would seem to lose a great deal of its value for them if it did not mean the establishment of their own personal sphere of influence, won at last after years of waiting and planning.

Well, suppose that a young wife has just managed to arrange her own household, and that she is proud of having done this, and that she is only just beginning to discover what she is like when she is captain of her own fate: what happens when she has a little child? I think that when she was pregnant she did not necessarily allow herself to think of the infant as a threat to her newly-found independence, because at that time there was so much else to think about. There is so much about the idea of having a baby that is exciting, interesting, and inspiring, and in any case she may have felt that the infant could be brought up to fit into her scheme of things and to enjoy growing up within her sphere of influence. So far so good, and no doubt she was right in thinking that her infant would take some of his pattern of culture and behaviour from the home he was born into. However, there is more to be said, and it is quite important.

Almost from the start the new baby has his own ideas; and if you have ten children you will not find two alike although they all grow up in the same home – your household. Ten children will see ten different mothers in you, and even one child will sometimes look your way and see you as loving and beautiful, but suddenly, for a few moments when the light is not good, or perhaps in the night when you go into his room because he is having a nightmare, will see you as a dragon or a witch, or something else that is terrible and dangerous.

The point is that each new child coming into your house brings with him his own view of the world, and a need to control his little bit of the world, and therefore each new child is a threat to your own set-up, your carefully constructed and well-maintained order of things. And knowing how much you value having your own way I am sorry for you.

Let me see if I can help. I think some of the difficulties that arise in this situation come from the fact that you tend to think that you like what you like because it is right, good and proper, best, cleverest, safest, quickest, most economical, and so on. No doubt you are often justified in so thinking, and a child can scarcely vie with you when it comes to a matter of skill and knowledge of the world. But the main point is that it is not because your way is best – it is because it is yours that you like it and trust it. That is the real reason why you want to dominate, and why shouldn't you? The house is yours, and that is why you married – partly. Besides, you may only feel safe when you have all the strings in your own hands.

Yes, you have every right to ask people in your own house to conform to your standards, to lay the breakfast things the way you have decided, grace before meat and no swearing;

but your right is based on the grounds that it is your house and that that is your way, and not because your way is best – though, to be sure, it may be.

Your own children may well expect you to know what you want, and what you believe in, and they will be helped by your faith, and will to a greater or lesser extent base their own standards on yours. But at the same time, and this is the point, do you not agree with me that the children themselves have their own beliefs and ideals, and of their own accord they seek order? Children do not like perpetual muddle or perpetual selfishness. Can you see that it must harm a child if you are so concerned with the establishment of your own rights in your own house that you fail to allow for the innate tendency of your infant and child to create a little world around himself that is his own affair and that has its own moral code? *If you are sufficiently confident about yourself* I think you will like to see how far you can let each of your children dominate the scene by his own impulses and schemes and ideas in a localized way, inside your wider influence. 'Today it's my birthday and so everything's my accord,' the little girl said, and this did not lead to chaos; it led to a day arranged not much unlike any other day, except that it was created by the child instead of by the mother, or nurse, or schoolmistress.

Of course, this is the sort of thing a mother ordinarily does at the beginning of the infant's life. Not being able to be entirely at the beck and call of her infant, she gives the breast at regular intervals, which is the next best thing, and she often succeeds in giving the baby a short period of illusion in which he does not have to recognize yet that a dream breast does not satisfy, however lovely the dream. He cannot get fat on a dream breast. That is to say, to be good the breast must also belong to mother, who is external to him and independent of him. It is not enough for baby to have the idea that he would like a feed; it is also necessary for mother to have the idea that she would like to feed him. To recognize this is a hard task for a child, and a mother can protect her infant from too early or too abrupt disillusionment.

At first, too, the baby is felt to be important. If he needs food or cries from discomfort, everything goes by the board until his needs have been attended to; and he is allowed as far as possible to be impulsive – for instance, making messes for no better reason than that he wants to. It seems a curious change from the infant's point of view, when mother becomes strict – sometimes suddenly becomes strict because she has been frightened by the neighbours – and starts what is called 'training', never relaxing till she has made her infant conform to her standard of cleanliness. She thinks she has done very well if her baby gives up all hope of retaining his valuable spontaneity and valuable impulsiveness. As a matter of fact, too early and too strict training in cleanliness often defeats its own ends, and a child clean at six months becomes defiantly or compulsively dirty, and exceedingly difficult to re-train. Fortunately, in many cases the child finds a way out and hope is not entirely lost; the spontaneity merely hides in a symptom such as bed-wetting. (As one watching, and not having to wash and dry the sheets, I have been delighted before now to find the child of a rather domineering mother bed-wetting, sticking to his guns though not exactly knowing what he is doing.) The reward is great for the mother who, while retaining her own values, can afford to wait for the child's own sense of values to develop.

If you let each child develop his own right to dominate you will be helping him. There will be the clash between your right to dominate and his, but this is natural and it is much better than imposing yourself on your child on the ground that you know best. You have a better reason – that you like your own way too. Let your child have a corner of the room or a cupboard or a bit of wall which is his or hers to mess or to tidy or to decorate, according to the child's mood, fancy, and whim. Each child of yours has a right to a bit of your house that he can call his own, and he also has a right to a bit of your time each day (and a bit of daddy's) on which he can count, and during which you are in his world. Of course the other extreme is not much use, when a mother, having no strong personal way of life herself, lets her child have all his own way. Then no one, not even the child, is happy.

Chapter 19

What Do We Mean by a
Normal Child?

We often talk about difficult children, and we try to describe and classify their difficulties; we also talk of normality, or health, but it is much harder to describe a normal child. We know well enough what we mean by normal when we are speaking of the body. We mean that the child's development is somewhere about average considering the child's age, and that there is no physical disease. We know, too, what we mean by a normal intellect. But a child with a healthy body, and a normal or even supra-normal intellect, can still be very far from normal as a whole personality.

We could think in terms of behaviour, comparing a child with other children of the same age, but we would hesitate before labelling children abnormal because of their behaviour, since there are such wide variations in the normal and, indeed, in what is expected; a child cries when hungry, and the question is, what is the age of the child? It is not abnormal to cry when hungry at a year old. A child takes a penny out of his mother's bag. Again, at what age? Most children of two would do this sometimes. Or watch two children who each act as if expecting to be hit; in one case there is no reality basis for the fear, whereas in the other, the child is always being hit at home. Or, a child is still feeding from the breast at three years old; this is very unusual in England, but in some parts of the world this is the custom. Not by comparing the behaviour of one child with another do we come to an understanding of what we mean by normal.

What we want to know is whether a child's personality is building up normally, and whether character is strengthening in a healthy way. Cleverness in a child will not make up for a hold-up in the maturing of the personality. If emotional development has got hung up at some spot, a child has to be going back whenever certain circumstances recur, to act as if still an infant or a little child. For instance, we say that someone is acting like a child if, whenever frustrated, that person changes into a nasty person, or has a heart attack. A so-called normal person has other ways of dealing with frustration.

I will try to say something positive about normal development. But first let us agree that the needs and feelings of infants are tremendously powerful. It is essential to look at the child as a human being who starts off with all the intense feelings of human beings, though his relation to the world is only beginning. People adopt all sorts of devices to try to recapture the feelings that belong to their own infancy and early childhood, feelings that are valuable because so intense.

On this assumption we may think of early childhood as a gradual process of the building up of belief. Belief in people and things is built up little by little through innumerable good experiences. 'Good' here means satisfactory enough, so that the need or the impulse can be said to have been met and justified. These good experiences are weighed against the bad experiences, 'bad' being the word we use when anger and hate and doubt turn up, as they inevitably do. Every human being has to find a place to operate from, and to build up there, in the self, an organization of the instinctive urges; every human being has to develop a personal method of living with these impulses in the particular kind of world which has been allotted him, and it is not easy. In fact, the main thing to point out to people about infants and children is that life for infants and children is not easy even if it has all sorts of good things about it, and there is no such thing as life without tears, except where there is compliance without spontaneity.

From this fact – that life is inherently difficult and that no infant or child can avoid showing evidence of its difficulties – it follows that in everyone there will be symptoms, any one of which, under certain conditions, could be a symptom of illness. Even the most kindly, understanding background of home-life cannot alter the fact that ordinary human development is hard, and indeed a perfectly adaptive home would be difficult to endure, because there would be no relief through justified anger.

So we are driven to the idea that there are two meanings to

the word normal. One is useful to the psychologist, who needs a standard, and who has to call everything abnormal that is imperfect. The other is useful to doctors, parents, and teachers when they want to describe a child who seems likely eventually to grow up into a satisfactory member of society, in spite of the fact that symptoms and inconvenient behaviour problems are clearly present.

For instance, I know a baby boy who was born prematurely. Doctors would say this was abnormal. He would not feed for ten days, so his mother had to express milk and give it in a bottle. This is normal for a premature child and abnormal for a full-term child. From the day when he ought to have been born he took the breast, although slowly, only at his own rate. From the beginning he made tremendous demands on his mother, who found she could succeed only by following him, letting him decide when to start and when to leave off. Throughout infancy he screamed at every new thing, and the only way to get him to use a new cup, or a new bath, or a cot, was to introduce him to it, and then to wait and wait till he turned to it. The degree to which he needed his own way spelt abnormality to a psychologist, but, because he had this mother who was willing to follow him, we can still call this child normal. As a further evidence of finding life difficult the child developed very intense screaming attacks, in which he got beyond being consoled, so that the only thing to do was to leave him in his cot and wait nearby till he recovered. In the attacks he did not know his mother, so she could not be of any use to him until he started to recover, when she became once more a mother he could use. The child was sent to a psychologist for special investigation, but while the mother was waiting for an appointment she found that the child and she together were becoming able to understand each other without help. The psychologist left them to it. He could see abnormality in the child and in the mother, but he preferred to call them normal, and to let them have the valuable experience of recovering from a difficult situation by means of their own natural resources.

For my own part, I use the following description of a normal child. A normal child *can* employ any or all of the devices nature has provided in defence against anxiety and intolerable conflict. The devices employed (in health) are related to the kind of help that is available. Abnormality shows in a *limitation* and a *rigidity* in the child's capacity to employ symptoms, and a relative lack of relationship between the symptoms and what can be expected in the way of help. Naturally, one has to allow for the fact that in earliest infancy there is but little capacity for judging what type of help is available, and a corresponding need for close adaptation on the part of the mother.

Take bed-wetting, a common enough symptom which almost everyone has to deal with who has to deal with children. If by bed-wetting a child is making effective protest against strict management, sticking up for the rights of the individual, so to speak, then the symptom is not an illness; rather it is a sign that the child still hopes to keep the individuality which has been in some way threatened. In the vast majority of cases, bed-wetting is doing its job, and given time, and with ordinary good management, the child will become able to leave off the symptom and adopt other methods of asserting the self.

Or take refusal of food – another common symptom. It is absolutely normal for a child to refuse food. I assume that the food you offer is good. The point really is that a child cannot always *feel* the food to be good. A child cannot *always* feel that good food is deserved. Given time and calm management the child will eventually find out what to call good, and what to call bad; in other words, will develop likes and dislikes, as we all do.

It is these devices that are normally employed by our children that we call symptoms, and we say that a normal child is able to have any kind of symptom in appropriate circumstances. But with an ill child it is not the symptoms that are the trouble; it is the fact that the symptoms are not doing their job, and are as much a nuisance to the child as to the mother.

So although bed-wetting, and refusal of food, and all sorts of other symptoms can be serious indications for treatment, they need not be so. In fact, children who can surely be called normal can be shown to have such symptoms, and to have them simply because life is difficult, inherently difficult for every human being, for every one from the very beginning.

From what do the difficulties arise? *Firstly*, there is the fundamental clash between the two kinds of reality, that of the external world which can be shared by everyone, and that of each child's personal inner world of feelings, ideas, imagination. From birth each baby is constantly being introduced to the fact of the external world. In the early feeding experiences, ideas are compared with fact; that which is wanted, expected, thought up, is weighed against what is supplied, against what is dependent for its existence on the will and wish of another person. Throughout life there must always be distress in connexion with this essential dilemma. Even the best external reality is disappointing because it is not also imaginary, and although perhaps to some extent it can be manipulated, it is not under magical control. One of the chief tasks before those who care for a little child is to give help in the painful transition from illusion to disillusion, by simplifying as far as possible the problem immediately in front of a child at any one moment. Much of the screaming and the temper tantrums of infancy range round this tug-of-war between inner and outer reality, and the tug-of-war must be reckoned normal.

A special part of this particular process of disillusionment is the child's discovery of the joy of the immediate impulse. If the child is to grow up, however, to join with the others of a group, a great deal of the joy that belongs to spontaneity has to be given up. Yet nothing can be given up that has not first been found and possessed. How difficult it is for the mother to make sure that each infant in turn gets the feeling of having had the essentials of love, before being asked to do with less than all! Clashes and protests are indeed to be expected normally in connexion with such painful learning.

Then, *secondly*, there is the awful discovery the infant begins to make that with excitement there go very destructive thoughts. When feeding, a child is liable to feel the urge to destroy everything that is good, the food, and the person who has the food to give him. This is very frightening, or gradually becomes so as the infant recognizes a person behind the child care, or because the child comes to be very fond of the person who at feed-times is there as if asking to be destroyed or used up. And, along with this, there comes a feeling that there will be nothing left if everything has been destroyed; and what happens then, should hunger return?

So what is to be done? Sometimes the child will just stop being eager about food, thereby gaining peace of mind but losing something valuable, because if there is no eagerness there cannot be the experience of full satisfaction. So here we have a symptom – inhibition of healthy greediness – which we must expect to some extent in children whom we shall call normal. If, in trying all sorts of dodges to get round the symptom, the mother knows what all the fuss is about, she will not be so liable to get in a panic and will be able to play for time, always a good thing in child care. It is wonderful what the human infant and child can manage in the end, because someone how is personally responsible is calmly and consistently continuing to act naturally.

All this only concerns the relation between the infant and the mother. Only too soon, added to other troubles, are those that belong to the child's recognition that there is also father to be reckoned with. A lot of the symptoms you note in your child have to do with the complications that arise naturally out of this fact and the wider implications. Yet we would not want there to be no father on this account. It is obviously better that all sorts of symptoms should appear as a direct result of a child's jealousy of the father, or love of him, or because of mixed feelings, than that the child should go straight ahead without having had to cope with this further hard fact of external reality.

And the arrival of new children causes upsets which likewise are desirable rather than deplorable.

And *lastly*, for I cannot mention everything, the child soon begins to create a personal inner world in which battles are lost and won, a world in which magic holds sway. From children's pictures and play you will see something of this inner world, which must be taken seriously. As this inner world seems to the child to have a position, seems to be located in the body, you must expect the child's body to be involved. For instance, all sorts of body pains and bodily upsets will accompany the strains and stresses in the inner world. And in an attempt to control inner phenomena a child will have aches and pains, or will make magic gestures, or dance round like one possessed, and I do not want you to think, when you have to deal with these 'mad' things in your own child, that the child is ill. You must expect a child to become possessed by all kinds of real and imaginary people, and by animals and things, and sometimes these imaginary people and animals will come outside, so that you will have to pretend you see them too, unless you want to cause great confusion through requiring your child to be grown-up while still a child. And do not be surprised if you have to cater for imaginary playmates who are entirely real to your child, derived from the inner world, yet for the time being kept external to the personality for some good reason.

Instead of going on trying to explain why life is normally difficult I will end with a friendly hint. Put a lot of store on a child's ability to play. If a child is playing there is room for a symptom or two, and if a child is able to enjoy play, both alone and with other children, there is no very serious trouble afoot. If in this play is employed a rich imagination, and if, also, pleasure is got from games that depend on exact perception of external reality, then you can be fairly happy, even if the child in question is wetting the bed, stammering, displaying temper tantrums, or repeatedly suffering from bilious attacks or depression. The playing shows that this child is capable, given reasonably good and stable surroundings, of developing a personal way of life, and eventually of becoming a whole human being, wanted as such, and welcomed by the world at large.

Chapter 20

The Only Child

I am going to discuss children who, although they live in ordinary good homes, have no brothers and sisters: only children. The question is: in what ways does it really matter whether a child is an only child or one of a family?

Now, when I look round and see so many only children I realize that there must be very good reasons for having only one. Of course, in many cases parents would do anything to have a large family, but something or other has cropped up which makes this impossible. But often there is a conscious plan to have no more than one child. I suppose the common reason given, if one asks why two married people intend to have only one child, is that it is a question of economics. 'We simply cannot afford more than one child.'

Babies undoubtedly are an expense. I think it would be most unwise to advise parents to ignore their inner promptings with regard to the financial side of family life. We all know of legitimate and illegitimate babies scattered all over the place by men and women with too little of that sense of responsibility which makes young people naturally hesitate before embarking on large families. If people like to speak in terms of money, let them, but really I think that what they doubt is whether they are able to support a large family without losing too much personal freedom. If two children do really make twice as much demand on mother and father as one child makes, then it is as well that the cost is counted in advance But one might doubt whether several children are, in fact, so much more of a burden than an only child can be.

Forgive me for calling a child a burden. Children *are* a burden, and if they bring joy it is because they are wanted, and two people have decided to take that kind of a burden; in fact, have agreed to call it not a burden, but a baby. There is a significant humorous saying: 'May all your troubles be little ones!' If we talk sentimentally about children people will give up having them altogether; mothers can enjoy washing and mending, but do not let us forget the work and the unselfishness it all means.

There are some undoubted advantages that a child can get out of being an only child. I think that the fact that the parents are able to devote themselves to the one baby means that it is possible for them to make better arrangements than they could otherwise do for that baby to have an uncomplicated infancy. That is to say, the baby can start with the simplest possible relationship between child and mother, and this bit of the world gradually develops complexity not faster than the developing infant can allow for. This foundation of existence in a simplified environment can give a sense of stability which can be a great stand-by for the whole of life. Also, of course, I should mention other important things, such as the food, clothing, and education which parents can easily give to their only child.

Now let me turn to some of the disadvantages. The obvious disadvantage of being an only child is the lack of playmates, and the lack of that richness of experience which can result from a child's various relationships to older and younger brothers and sisters. There is much in the play of children which grown-ups cannot get into touch with; even if they understand it, they cannot enter into it for such long periods as the child would like. In fact, if grown-ups play with a child the natural madness in the child's play becomes too evident. So, if there are no other children, a child becomes stunted in play and misses the pleasures that belong to inconsequence, irresponsibility, and impulsiveness; the tendency is for the only child to become precocious, and to prefer listening and talking in grown-up company and helping mother about the house, or using father's tools. It becomes silly to play. Children who play together have an infinite capacity for inventing play-details, and they also go on playing for long periods without tiring.

But I think there is something even more important; it is valuable for a child to experience the entry of a new brother or sister into the family. In fact, I cannot over-emphasize the value of this experience. There is something quite fundamental in the fact of pregnancy, and a child has missed a great deal who has missed seeing the changes in his mother, finding himself unable to be comfortable on her lap, gradually coming to the reason for this, and getting tangible proof of what he secretly knows all the time in the eventual appearance of the new baby, and the simultaneous return of mother to normal. Even if there are many children who find this rather strong meat, and who fail to cope with the tremendous feelings and conflicts aroused, nevertheless it remains true, I think, that every child who has missed such an experience, and who has never seen mother giving milk from her breasts, and bathing and caring for an infant, is less rich than the child who has witnessed these things. And perhaps little children wish to have babies as much as grown-ups do. But they cannot, and dolls only partly satisfy them. By proxy they can have children if their mother has them.

One thing the only child especially lacks is the experience of finding hate turn up; the child's own hate, as the new baby threatens what seemed to be a settled and safe relation to the mother and father. It is so usual as to be called normal when a child is upset at the birth of a new one. The child's first comment is not usually polite: 'It's got a face like a tomato'; in fact parents should feel relieved when they hear the direct expression of conscious dislike, and even violent hate, at the birth of a new child. This hate will gradually give way to love as the new infant develops into a human being, who can be played with, and of whom one can be proud. The first reaction, however, can be of fear and hate and the impulse may be to put the new baby in the dustbin. I think that it is a very valuable experience for a child to find that the younger brother or sister for whom love is beginning to develop is the same as the new baby who was hated a few weeks ago and actually wished away. For all children a big difficulty is the legitimate expression of hate, and the only child's relative lack of opportunity for expressing the aggressive side of his nature is a serious thing. Children who grow up together play games of all kinds, and so have a chance to come to terms with their own aggressiveness, and they have valuable opportunities for discovering on their own that they mind when they really hurt someone they love.

Another thing, the arrival of new babies means that father and mother are still sexually interested in each other as well as fond of each other. I personally think that children get valuable reassurance about the relations between father and mother through the advent of new babies; and it is always vitally important to children that they should be able to feel that mother and father are sexually drawn together, maintaining the structure of family life.

A family of children has one other advantage over an only child. In a big family there is a chance for children to play all sorts of different roles in relation to each other, and all this prepares them for life in larger groups and eventually in the world. Only children as they grow older, especially if they have not many cousins, find it difficult to meet other boys and girls on a casual basis. Only children are all the time looking for *stable* relationships and this tends to scare off the casual acquaintance, whereas the members of large families are used to meeting the friends of their brothers and sisters, and they have a good deal of practical experience of human relationships by the time they reach the age of dating.

Parents can certainly do a very great deal for an only child, and many prefer to do their best in this way, but they also stand to suffer. In war-time especially they have to be very brave to let their child go and fight, although it may be the only good thing from the child's point of view. Boys and girls need the freedom to run risks, and it is a serious frustration to them if they cannot do so because, being only children, they may hurt their parents too much if they themselves get hurt. There is also the fact that a man and woman are enriched by every child they nurture and launch into the world.

Furthermore, there is the matter of the care of father and mother as the child grows older. When there are several children the care of father and mother can be shared. Clearly, only children can be weighed down by their own wish to look after their parents. Perhaps parents ought to think of this in advance. They sometimes forget that when they looked after the child, the child quickly grew up and was young only for a few years. But the child may be looking after the parents (and may want to do so) for twenty or thirty years, or more; always an indefinite period. If there are several children it is much easier for the care of ageing parents to remain a pleasure to the end. As a matter of fact, it sometimes happens that young married people who would like to have several children are unable to do so because they have the great responsibility of their ageing or ill parents who did not have enough children to enable this work to be shared, and so enjoyed.

You will notice that I have discussed the advantages and disadvantages of being an only child on the assumption that the child is an ordinary healthy, normal individual, with an ordinary good home. Obviously a great deal more could be said if one were to think of abnormalities. For instance, parents who have a backward child have a special problem which deserves special consideration, and many children are so difficult to manage that parents naturally wonder whether other children would be harmed by the one difficult child, and by the type of management which this child forces them to adopt. And then there is the equally important case of the child whose parents are in some way or other ill – either physically or psychologically. For instance, some mothers and fathers are more or less always depressed, or they worry; some are so frightened of the world that they build their home on the basis that the world is hostile to it. An only child has to discover this and deal with it all alone. As a friend said to me, 'For me there was an odd feeling of closed-in-ness; perhaps too much love, too much attention, too much possessiveness made one feel shut up with these parents who imagined, long after it had ceased to be true, that they were the whole of one's world. For me this was infinitely the worst part of being an only child. My parents were outwardly wise about the matter. They sent me to school when I could hardly walk, and let me practically live with the children next door, but at home there was this odd drawing-in as though family ties were infinitely more important than others. If there is no one in the family who is one's contemporary, all this is apt to fill a child with a kind of pride.'

You will have gathered that in my personal opinion there are more arguments in favour of the large family than in favour of the only child. However, it is much better to have one or two children, and to do one's best for the few, than to have an unlimited number without the physical strength and the emotional stamina to cope with them. If there must be one child in a family and no more, let it be remembered that other people's children can be invited to the house, and that this can start early. And the fact that two little children bang each other on the head does not mean they ought not to have met. When there are no children available there can be dogs and other pets, and there are nursery schools and kindergartens. If the immense disadvantages of being an only child are understood, they can be got round to some extent, provided the will to get round them exists.

Chapter 21

Twins

The first thing to say about twins is that they are perfectly natural phenomena, and really nothing to be sentimental or facetious about. I know many mothers who have loved having twins, and I know many twins who have liked being twins. But nearly all mothers say they would not have actually chosen twins had they been asked, and twins, even those who seem quite contented with their lot, usually tell me they would have preferred to have come one at a time.

Twins have their own particular problems to solve. Whatever the advantages of being a twin, there are also disadvantages. If I can help, it will be not so much by telling you what to do as by giving you a hint or two of the main difficulty.

There are two different sorts of twins, and the problem is not exactly the same for each kind. You know that every baby develops from one minute cell, a fertilized ovum or egg cell. As soon as the ovum is fertilized it starts growing, and it divides into two. Each of these two cells divides into two, making four, and the four become eight, and this goes on till the new individual is made up of millions of cells of all types, all related to each other, and as much a unity as was the original fertilized ovum. Sometimes, after the first division of the newly-fertilized ovum, each of the two cells divides and then develops independently, and this is the beginning of the identical twins: two babies developing from the same fertilized ovum. Identical twins are always of the same sex, and they are usually very much like each other in appearance, at least at first.

The other kind of twins may or may not be of the same sex, as they are just like any other brothers and sisters, except that they developed from ova that happened to be fertilized at the same moment. The two ova in this case grow side by side in the womb. Twins of this kind do not necessarily look alike, any more than other brothers and sisters do.

Looking at twins of either kind we easily feel that it must be nice for each child to have company – never to be alone, especially as the two get older. There is a snag, however, and to understand this we have to remind ourselves of the way that infants develop. In ordinary circumstances, and with ordinary good management, infants start immediately after birth to form the basis of their personalities and of their individuality, and to discover their own importance. We all like unselfishness and a willingness to allow for the other person's point of view, and hope to find these virtues in our children, but, if we study the emotional development of the infant, we find that unselfishness only comes in a healthy and stable way if it is based on a primary experience of selfishness. It might be said that without this *primary selfishness* a child's unselfishness gets clogged up with resentment. Anyway, this primary selfishness is no more than the infant's experience of good mothering, a good mother being willing, at first, to fit in with her baby's desires as far as possible, letting the baby's impulses dominate the situation, and being contented to wait for the baby's ability to allow for the other person's point of view to develop in the course of time. At the start a mother must be able to give her baby the sense of possession, and the feeling that he has control over her, the feeling that she has been created for the occasion. Her own private life is not forced on the baby at first. With the experience of primary selfishness in his bones the baby will be able to become unselfish later without too much resentment.

Now, in the ordinary way, when babies come singly, each little human being can take what time is needed to recognize the right of his mother to other interests, and it is well known that every child finds the arrival of a new child a complication, sometimes quite a serious one. No mother would worry if her baby failed to appreciate the benefits of the companionship of other babies till well after the first birthday, and even two-year-olds may bash each other rather than play together, at first. For indeed each baby has his own time for welcoming a brother or sister; and it is an important moment when a little child can genuinely 'allow' (that is, give) his mother a new pregnancy.

Now, the twin always has another baby to cope with, quite apart from the development of any willingness to allow an addition to the family.

This is one of the times when we see the fallacy of the view that little things do not matter in the early months, because it matters very much whether twins do, or do not, feel that they each had possession of mother at the start. The mother of twins has an extra task on top of everything else, which is to give the whole of herself to two babies at once. To some extent she must fail, and the mother of twins must be content to do her best, and hope that the children will eventually find advantages that will compensate for this inherent disadvantage of the twin state.

It is impossible for one mother to meet two infants' immediate needs at once. For instance, she cannot take up each of two children first, whether to feed them, or to change their napkins, or to bath them. She can try very hard to be fair, and it will repay her if she takes this matter seriously from the beginning, but it cannot be easy.

As a matter of fact she will find her aim is not to treat each child alike, but to treat each child as if that one were the only one. That is to say, she will be trying to find the differences between each infant from the moment of birth. She, of all people, must know each from the other easily, even if she has to tell one at first by a little mark on the skin, or by some other trick. She will usually come to find that the two temperaments are different, and that if she easily acts in relation to each as a total personality, each will develop personal characteristics. It is thought that a lot of the difficulty about twins arises out of the fact that they are not always recognized as different from each other, even where they are different, either because of the fun of it, or because there is no one who thinks this task worth the trouble. I know of a quite good home in which the matron never managed to learn to distinguish between two twin girls, although the other children had no difficulty in knowing one from the other; in fact the two girls really had quite distinct personalities. The matron used to call each one 'Twin'.

It is no solution to look after one yourself and to hand the other over to a nurse. You might have to share the care of the children with someone else for some good reason, if you are not in good health, for instance; but then you will not do more than postpone things, because one day the twin you handed over is going to be very jealous of the one you kept, even if the better mothering was done by the helper.

Mothers of twins seem to agree that even when the twins enjoy at times being mistaken for each other, these same children need their own mother to recognize the identity of each without trouble. It is essential in every case that there should be no confusion among the children themselves, and for that there must be some person in their lives who is quite clear about them. A mother I know had identical twins, exactly alike to outsiders, but distinguished easily by their mother from the beginning, because of their temperaments. In the first week or so this mother complicated her feeding routine by wearing a red shawl. One twin reacted to this, and simply gazed at the shawl – perhaps at its bright colour – and lost interest in the breast. The other, however, was unaffected by the shawl, and fed as usual. After this the mother felt not only that the two were two persons, but also that they had already ceased living parallel experiences. This particular mother got round the who-to-feed-first difficulty by having the feeds ready well on time, and feeding first the infant that seemed more eager. It was usually easy to decide by the crying. I do not say this method would suit all cases.

Certainly the main complication in the upbringing of twins is this question of the personal treatment and management of each, so that the wholeness and oneness of each gets full re-cognition. Even if there were twins that were exactly alike there would still be the need for their own mother to have a whole relation to each.

The mother I spoke about just now told me she found it a good idea to put one baby to sleep in the front garden, and the other in the back. Of course, you may not happen to have two gardens, but you may be able to arrange things somehow so that when one infant cries you will not always have to have the two crying. Not only is it a pity from your point of view to have the two at it at once, but also when crying a baby likes to dominate the scene; it is maddening to have a rival in early infancy at the stage of natural dictatorship, and I have known the effects of this sort of thing persist long into a twin's life.

I said that twins of one kind are called identical twins. Surely this word gives the whole show away. If the children *were* identical they would each be the same, they would add up to one, so to speak, which is absurd. They are similar, but not identical; the danger is that people will treat them as identical, and as I have said, if people do this the twins will themselves feel muddled about their own identities. And infants do become very muddled about their own identities apart from being twins; it is only gradually that they become sure of themselves. As you know, it is quite a while after words are used that children use pronouns. They say 'mum' and 'dad' and 'more' and 'dog' long before they say 'I' and 'you' and 'we'. It is quite possible for twins to sit in a pram, each thinking the other is not a separate person. Indeed, it would be more natural for an infant to think it to be himself at the other end of the pram (rather like looking in a mirror) than to say (in infant language) 'hullo, there's my twin opposite me'. But when one gets lifted out of the pram the other feels lost and cheated. Here is a difficulty that any baby may have, but that twins *must* have, and they can only hope to manage if we play our part, and know them as two people. Later, if the twins themselves become quite confident about their identities they may enjoy exploiting their likeness to each other, and then, and not before then, is the time for fun and games on the theme of mistaken identity.

Finally, do twins like each other? This is a question that twins must answer. From what I am told, I feel that the idea that twins are specially fond of each other needs looking into. Often they accept each other's company, enjoy playing together, and hate to be separated, and yet fail to convince one that they love each other. Then one day they discover that they hate each other like poison, and at last the possibility that they may get to love each other has come. This will not fit all cases, but where two children have had to put up with each other willy-nilly they cannot know whether they would have chosen to know each other. After the hate is expressed, the love has a chance. So it is important that you should not take it too much for granted that your twins will want to spend their lives together.

They may, but they may not, and they may even be grateful to you, or to some chance thing like measles, for separating them, it being much easier to become a whole person alone than in company with one's twin.

Chapter 22

Why Children Play

Why do children play? Here are some of the reasons, obvious, but perhaps worth reviewing.

Most people would say that children play because they like doing so, and this is undeniable. Children enjoy all physical and emotional play experiences. We can increase the range of both kinds of their experiences by providing materials and ideas, but it seems to be better to provide too little rather than too much of these commodities, since children are able to find objects and invent games very easily, and they enjoy doing so.

It is commonly said that children 'work off hate and aggression' in play, as if aggression were some bad substance that could be got rid of. This is partly true, because pent-up resentment and the results of angry experience can feel to a child like bad stuff inside himself. But it is more important to state this same thing by saying that the child values finding that hate or aggressive urges can be expressed in a known environment, without the return of hate and violence from the environment to the child. A good environment, the child would feel, should be able to tolerate aggressive feelings if they are expressed in more or less acceptable form. It must be accepted that aggression is there, in the child's make-up, and the child feels dishonest if what is there is hidden and denied.

Aggression can be pleasurable, but it inevitably carries with it a real or imagined hurting of someone, so that the child cannot avoid having to deal with this complication. To some extent this is dealt with at source, by the child's accepting the discipline of expressing the aggressive feeling in play form and not just when angry. Another way is for aggression to be used in activity that has ultimate constructive aim. But these things are only gradually achieved. It is our part to see that we do not ignore the social contribution the child makes by expressing his aggressive feelings in play instead of at the moment of rage. We may not like being hated or hurt, but we must not ignore what underlies self-discipline in regard to angry impulses.

Whereas it is easy to see that children play for pleasure, it is much more difficult for people to see that children play to master anxiety, or to master ideas and impulses that lead to anxiety if they are not in control.

Anxiety is always a factor in a child's play, and often it is a major factor. Threat of excess of anxiety leads to compulsive play, or to repetitive play, or to an exaggerated seeking for the pleasures that belong to play; and if anxiety is too great, play breaks down into pure exploitation of sensual gratification.

This is not the place to prove the thesis that anxiety underlies children's play. The practical result, however, is important. For in so far as children only play for pleasure they can be asked to give it up, whereas, in so far as play deals with anxiety, we cannot keep children from it without causing distress, actual anxiety, or new defences against anxiety (such as masturbation or day-dreaming).

The child gains experience in play. Play is a big part of his life. External as well as internal experiences can be rich for the adult, but for the child the riches are to be found chiefly in play and fantasy. Just as the personalities of adults develop through their experience in living, so those of children develop through their own play, and through the play inventions of other children and of adults. By enriching themselves children gradually enlarge their capacity to see the richness of the externally real world. Play is the continuous evidence of creativity, which means aliveness.

Grown-ups contribute here by recognizing the big place of play, and by teaching traditional games, yet without cramping or corrupting the children's own inventiveness.

Children at first play alone, or with mother; other children are not immediately in demand as playmates. It is largely through play, in which the other children are fitted into preconceived roles, that a child begins to allow these others to have independent existence. Just as some adults make friends and enemies easily at work whereas others may sit in a boarding-house for years and do no more than wonder why no one seems to want them, so do children make friends and enemies during play, while they do not easily make friends apart from play. Play provides an organization for the initiation of emotional relationships, and so enables social contacts to develop.

Play, and the use of art forms, and religious practice, tend in various but allied ways towards a unification and general integration of the personality. For instance, play can easily be seen to link the individual's relation to inner reality with the same individual's relation to external or shared reality.

In another way of looking at this highly complex matter, it is in play that the child links ideas with bodily function. It would be profitable, in this connexion, to examine masturbation or other sensual exploitation along with the conscious and unconscious fantasy that belongs to it, and to compare this with true playing, in which conscious and unconscious ideas hold sway, and the related bodily activities are either in abeyance or else are harnessed to the play content.

It is when one comes across a case of a child whose compulsive masturbation is *apparently* free of fantasy, or on the other hand a child whose compulsive day-dreaming is *apparently* free from either localized or general bodily excitement, that we recognize most clearly the healthy tendency that there is in play which relates the two aspects of life to each other, bodily functioning and the aliveness of ideas. Play is the alternative to sensuality in the child's effort to keep whole. It is well known that when anxiety is relatively great sensuality becomes compulsive, and play becomes impossible.

Similarly, when one meets with a child in whom the relation to inner reality is unjoined to the relation to external reality, in other words, whose personality is seriously divided in this respect, we see most clearly how normal playing (like the remembering and telling of dreams) is one of the things that tend towards integration of personality. The child with such serious splitting of the personality cannot play, or cannot play in ways that are generally recognizable. Today (1968) I would add four comments:

(1) Playing is essentially creative. (2) Playing is always exciting because it deals with the existence of a precarious borderline between the subjective and that which can be objectively perceived. (3) Playing takes place in the potential space between the baby and the mother-figure. This potential space belongs to the change that has to be taken into consideration when the baby who is merged in with the mother feels the mother to be separated off. (4) Playing develops in this potential space according to the opportunity that the baby has to experience separation without separation, this being possible because the state of being merged in with the mother is replaced by the mother's adaptation to the baby's needs. In other words, the initiation of playing is associated with the life experience of the baby who has come to trust the mother-figure.

Play can be 'a being honest about oneself', just as dressing can be for an adult. This can become changed at an early age into its opposite, for play, like speech, can be said to be given us to hide our thoughts, if it is the deeper thoughts that we mean. The repressed unconscious must be kept hidden, but the rest of the unconscious is something that each individual wants to get to know, and play, like dreams, serves the function of self-revelation.

In psychoanalysis of little children, the desire to communicate through play is used in place of the adult's speaking. The three-year-old child often has a great belief in our capacity to understand so that the psychoanalyst has difficulty in living up to what the child expects. Great bitterness can follow the child's disillusionment in this respect, and there could be no greater stimulus to the analyst in the search for deeper understanding than the child's distress at our failure to understand what he or she communicates through play.

Older children are comparatively disillusioned in this respect, and it is no great shock to them to be misunderstood, or even to find that they can deceive, and that education is largely education in deception and compromise. However, all children (even some adults) remain to a lesser or greater degree capable of regaining the belief in being understood, and in their play we can always find the gateway to the unconscious, and to the native honesty which so curiously starts in full bloom in the infant, and then unripens to a bud.

Chapter 23

The Child and Sex

Only a little while ago it was thought bad to link sex with childhood 'innocence'. At the present time the need is for accurate description. As so much is as yet unknown the student is recommended to carry out research in his own way, and if he must read instead of making observations let him read descriptions by many different writers, not looking to one or another as the purveyor of the truth. This chapter is not the retailing of a set of theories bought wholesale, it is an attempt to put in a few words one person's description of childhood sexuality, based on his training and experience as a paediatrician and psychoanalyst. The subject is vast, and cannot be confined to the limits of a chapter without suffering distortion.

In considering any aspect of child psychology it is useful to remember that everyone has been a child. In each adult observer there is the whole memory of his infancy and childhood, both the fantasy and the reality, in so far as it was appreciated at the time. Much is forgotten but nothing is lost. What better example could direct attention to the vast resources of the unconscious!

In oneself, it is possible to sort out from the vast unconscious the repressed unconscious, and this will include some sexual elements. If special difficulty is found in allowing even for the possibility of childhood sexuality, it is better to turn one's attention to another subject. On the other hand, the observer who is reasonably free to find what is to be observed, not having to guard too much (for personal reasons) against finding whatever is to be found, can choose from many different methods for objective study! The most fruitful, and therefore the one necessary for anyone who intends to make psychology his life work, is personal analysis, in which (if it is successful) he not only loses the active repressions, but also discovers through memory, and by reliving, the feelings and essential conflicts of his own early life.

Freud, who was responsible for drawing attention to the importance of childhood sexuality, arrived at his conclusions through the analysis of adults. The analyst has a unique experience every time he conducts a successful analysis, in that he sees unfolding before him the patient's childhood and infancy as it appeared to the patient. He has the repeated experience of getting to see the natural history of a psychological disorder, with all the interweaving of the psychological and the physical, of the personal and the environmental, of the factual and the imagined, of what has been conscious to the patient and what has been under repression.

In analysis of adults Freud found that the foundations of their sex life and sex difficulties went back to adolescence, and back to childhood, especially to the two- to five-year-old period.

He found that there was a triangular situation which could not be described except by saying that the little boy was in love with his mother, and was in conflict with his father as a sexual rival. The sexual element was proved by the fact that it was not just in fantasy that these things were happening; there were physical accompaniments, erections, excitement phases with climax, murderous impulses, and a specific fear – fear of castration. This central theme was picked out and called the Oedipus complex, and it remains today a central fact, infinitely elaborated and modified, but inescapable. Psychology built on a hushing up of this central theme would have been doomed to failure, and therefore one cannot help being grateful to Freud for going ahead and stating what he repeatedly found, bearing the brunt of public reaction.

In using the term 'Oedipus complex' Freud paid tribute to the intuitive understanding of childhood which is independent of psychoanalysis. The Oedipus myth really shows that what Freud wanted to describe has always been known.

A tremendous development of theory has taken place round the nucleus of the Oedipus complex, and much of the criticism of the idea would have been justified if the theory had been put forward as an artist's intuitive understanding of the whole of childhood sexuality or of psychology. But the concept was like a rung in a ladder of scientific procedure. As a concept it had the great merit that it dealt with both the physical and the imaginative. Here was a psychology in which the body and the mind were simply two aspects of one person, essentially related and not to be examined separately without loss of value.

If the central fact of the Oedipus complex is accepted it is immediately possible and desirable to examine the ways in which the concept is inadequate or inaccurate as a clue to child psychology.

The first objection comes from direct observation of little boys. Some boys do express in so many words and quite openly their in-love feeling for their mother and their wish to marry her, and even to give her children, and their consequent hate of father; but many do not express themselves in this way at all, and in fact seem to have more love feeling towards father than towards mother; and in any case brothers and sisters, nurses, and aunts and uncles, easily take the place of the parents. Direct observation does not confirm the degree of importance given to the Oedipus complex by the psychoanalyst. Nevertheless, the psychoanalyst must stick to his guns, because in analysis he regularly finds it, and regularly finds it to be important, and often he finds it severely repressed and only emerging after most careful and prolonged analysis. If, in the observation of children, their games are intimately examined, sexual themes and the Oedipus theme will be regularly found among all the others; but again, the intimate examination of children's games is difficult, and is best done in the course of analysis if it is carried out for research purposes.

The fact seems to be that the full Oedipus situation is but seldom enacted openly in real life. Intimations of it there certainly are, but the tremendously intense feelings associated with periods of instinctual excitement are largely in the child's unconscious or quickly become repressed, being nonetheless real for all that; temper attacks and the common nightmares that occur normally in the three-year-old cannot be understood except in terms of firm attachment to persons, with periodically rising instinctual tension, and acute exacerbation of conflict in the mind arising out of hate and fear clashing with love.

149

A modification of the original idea (one made by Freud himself) is that the very intense and highly coloured sex situations that an adult in analysis recovers from his own childhood are not necessarily episodes that could have been observed as such by his parents, but nevertheless are true reconstructions based on unconscious feelings and ideas belonging to childhood.

This brings up another point, what about little girls? The first assumption was that they fall in love with their fathers, and hate and fear their mothers. Here again is a truth, and here again the main part is likely to be unconscious, not something that the little girl would admit, except in very special circumstances of trust.

Many girls, however, do not get so far in their emotional development as to become attached to father, and to take the very great risks inherent in being in conflict with mother. Alternatively, an attachment to father is formed, but regression (as it is called) occurs back from a weakly acquired relation to father. The risks inherent in conflict with mother are great indeed, for with the idea of mother (in unconscious fantasy) is associated the idea of loving care, good food, the stability of the earth, and the world in general; and a conflict with mother necessarily involves a feeling of insecurity, and dreaming of the ground opening, or worse. The little girl, then, has a special problem, if only because when she comes to love her father her rivalry is with her mother, who is her first love in a more primitive way.

The little girl, like the little boy, has physical sex feelings appropriate to the type of fantasy. It might usefully be said that whereas a boy at the height of his sex wave (at the toddler age and at puberty) is especially afraid of castration, in a girl at a corresponding stage the trouble is a conflict in her relation to the physical world brought about by her rivalry with her mother, who was originally for the child the physical world itself. At the same time the little girl suffers fears in regard to her body, fears of castration like those of a boy, and fears that her body will be attacked by hostile mother figures, in retaliation for her wish to steal her mother's babies, and much else.

This description is obviously defective in respect of bisexuality. At the same time in a child's life that the ordinary heterosexual relationship is vitally important the homosexual relationship always exists, and can be relatively more important than the other. Another way of putting this is to say that a child normally becomes identified with each parent, but at any one moment principally with one parent; and this parent need not be the one of the child's sex. In all cases there is a capacity for identification with the parent of the other sex, so that in the sum total of a child's fantasy life (if search be made) there can be found the whole range of relationships, regardless of the actual sex of the child. It is convenient, naturally, when the main identification is with the parent of the same sex, but in psychiatric examination of a child it would be wrong to jump to a diagnosis of abnormality if the finding is that the child is mainly wanting to be like the parent of the other sex. Such can be the child's natural adaptation to special circumstances. In certain cases cross-identifications can, of course, be a basis for later homosexual tendencies of abnormal quality. In the 'latency' period, between the first sexual period and adolescence, cross-identifications are especially important.

A principle is being taken for granted in this description which perhaps ought to be deliberately formulated. The basis of sexual health is laid down in childhood, and in the reduplication of early childhood development that takes place at puberty. The corollary is equally true, that sexual aberrations and abnormalities of adult life are laid down in early childhood. Further, the basis of the whole of mental health is laid in early childhood and in infancy.

Ordinarily a child's play is greatly enriched by sexual ideas and sexual symbolism, and if there is strong sex-inhibition a play-inhibition follows. There is a possible confusion here arising out of the lack of clear definition of sex play. Sexual excitement is one thing, and the acting out of sex fantasy is another. Sex play with bodily excitement is a special case, and in childhood the outcome is liable to be difficult. The climax or detumescence is often represented more by the aggressive outburst that follows frustration than by a true relief of instinctual tension such as can be obtained by an older person after the onset of puberty. In sleep the dream life rises at times to excited states, and at the climax the body commonly finds some substitute for full sexual orgasm, such as wetting, or waking in nightmare. Sexual orgasm is not likely to be as satisfactory, as such, in the little boy as it can be after puberty, with emission added; perhaps it is more easily got by the little girl who has nothing to add as she matures, except being penetrated. These times of recurring instinctual tension must be expected in childhood, and substitute climaxes have to be provided – notably meals – but also parties, outings, special moments.

Parents know well enough that they often have to step in and induce a climax by a show of strength, even a smack producing tears. Mercifully, children get tired in the end, and go to bed and sleep. Even so, the delayed climax may disturb the calm of night, as the child wakes in a night-terror, and mother or father is needed immediately if the child is to regain a relation to external reality, and the relief that comes from an appreciation of what is stable in the real world.

All physical excitements have ideational accompaniments, or (the other way round) ideas are themselves the accompaniment of physical experience. Mental pleasure, as well as gratification and relief from tension, comes from the common playing of childhood which is the acting out of fantasy apart from physical excitement. Much of the normal and healthy play of childhood is concerned with sexual ideas and symbolism; this is not saying that children who are playing are always sexually excited. Children, when playing, may get excited in a general way, and periodically the excitement can become localized and therefore obviously sexual, or urinary, or greedy, or something else based on the capacity of tissues for excitement. Excitement calls for climax. The obvious way out for a child is the game with climax, in which excitement leads to something, 'a chopper to chop off your head', a forfeit, a prize, someone is caught or killed, someone has won, and so on.

Innumerable examples could be given of sex fantasy acted out, but not necessarily accompanied by bodily excitement. It is well known that a big proportion of little girls and some little boys like to play with dolls and to act towards the dolls as mothers do towards babies. They not only do as mother did, thereby complimenting her, but also they do as mother ought to have done, thereby reproaching her. The identification with a mother can be very complete and detailed. As in all these matters, there is a physical side of the experience along with the fantasy that is being acted out, and pains in the belly and sickness can be due to the mother game. Boys as well as girls stick their bellies out for fun, imitating pregnant women, and it is not very uncommon for a child to be brought to the doctor for enlarged belly when the trouble is a secret imitation of a pregnant woman, whose condition is supposed to have been unnoticed. As a matter of fact children are always looking out for swellings, and however successfully sex information is withheld from them they are unlikely to miss spotting a pregnancy. They may, however, keep the information in a compartment of the mind, unassimilated, because of the parents' prudery, or their own sense of guilt.

Children the world over have a game called 'Fathers and Mothers', which becomes enriched by an infinite quantity of imaginative material, and the pattern each group of children evolves tells a good deal about the children, and especially about the dominant personality in the group.

Children do often act out the adult type of sexual relationship in relation to each other, but usually this is done secretly and is not therefore recorded by people who are making deliberate observations. Naturally, children easily feel guilty in so playing and also they cannot help being affected by the fact that such play comes under a social ban. It could not be said that these sexual incidents are harmful, but if they are accompanied by a feeling of severe guilt and become repressed, unavailable to the child's consciousness, then harm has been done. This harm can be undone by the recovery of the memory of the incident, and it can sometimes be said that such an incident easily remembered has its value as a stepping-stone in the long and difficult journey from immaturity to maturity.

There are many other sex games which are related less directly to sexual fantasy. No claim is made here that children think only of sex: however, a sex-inhibited child is a poor companion, and is impoverished, like a sex-inhibited adult.

The subject of childhood sexuality simply does not allow itself to be confined rigidly to the excitement of sex organs and the fantasy that belongs to such excitement. In studying childhood sexuality it is possible to see the way in which the more specific excitement is built up out of bodily excitements of all types, reaching forward to the more mature feelings and ideas easily recognized as sexual; the more mature develops from the more primitive, the sexual from (for instance) the cannibalistic instinctual urges.

It can be said that a capacity for sexual excitement, in either sex, is present from birth, but the primary capacity of parts of the body for excitement has limited significance until the child's personality has become integrated and it can be said that it is the child as a whole person who is excited in that specific way. As the infant develops, the sexual type of excitement gradually acquires importance relative to the other types of excitement (urethral, anal, skin, oral), and at the age of three, four, or five years (as also at puberty) becomes capable, in healthy development, of dominating over other functions in appropriate circumstances.

This is another way of saying that all the innumerable accompaniments of sex in adult behaviour derive from early childhood, and it would be an abnormality and an impoverishment if an adult could not naturally and unselfconsciously employ all manner of infantile or 'pregenital' techniques in sex play. Nevertheless, the compulsion to employ a pregenital *instead of* genital technique in sex experience constitutes perversion, and has its origin in a hold-up of emotional development in early childhood. In analysis of a case of perversion there can always be found both a fear in regard to forward development to mature sex, and a special capacity to get satisfaction in more primitive ways. Sometimes there are actual experiences enticing the child back to infantile types of experience (as when an infant has become excited at introduction of a suppository, or has reacted with excitement to being tightly bound by a nurse, and so on).

The story of the building up of the mature child from the immature infant is long and complex, also it is vitally important for the understanding of the psychology of the adult human being. To develop naturally, the infant and child need a relatively stable environment.

Roots of Female Sexuality. The roots of a little girl's sexuality go right down to her early greedy feelings in relation to her mother. There is a gradation from her hungry attack on her mother's body to the mature wish to be like mother. Her love of her father can be as much determined by his being stolen (so to speak) from mother as by his actually being especially loving to her; indeed, when a father is away over the period of a girl's infancy so that she does not really know him, her choice of him as a love object may be entirely due to the fact that he is mother's man. For these reasons there is a close association between stealing and sex desire, and the wish to have a baby.

The consequence of this is that when a woman becomes pregnant and has a baby she has to be able to deal with the feeling, somewhere in her, that the baby was stolen from inside her mother's body. If she cannot feel this, as well as knowing the facts, she loses something of the gratification that pregnancy can bring, and she loses much of the special joy of presenting her own mother with a grandchild. This idea of theft can cause guilt after conception, and can cause miscarriage.

It is especially important to know of this guilt potential in the practical matter of management of the period immediately after childbirth. A mother is at that time very sensitive to the type of woman in charge of her and her baby. She needs help, but because of these ideas derived from early childhood she can only believe in a very friendly or a very hostile mother-figure at that time; and a mother having her first baby, even if she is healthy-minded, is very liable to feel persecuted by her nurse. The reason for this and other phenomena characteristic of the state of motherhood must be sought in the early roots of the little girl's relation to mother, including her primitive wish to gain womanliness by tearing it from her mother's body.

Here is another principle that is worth formulating: in psychiatry every abnormality is a disturbance of emotional development. In treatment, a cure is brought about by enabling the patient's emotional development to go ahead where it was held up. To get to this point where it is held up the patient must always get back to early childhood or infancy, and this fact ought to be of extreme importance to the paediatrician.

Psychosomatic Disorders. There is one way in which childhood sexuality is of direct importance to the practising paediatrician: that is, the transformation of sexual excitement into symptoms and physiological changes that resemble the symptoms and changes brought about by physical diseases. These symptoms, which are called psychosomatic, are exceedingly common in all medical practice, and it is from them that the general practitioner weeds out the occasional textbook diseases for the expert attention of the specialist in physical disease.

These psychosomatic disorders are not seasonal or epidemic; in any one child, however, they show a periodicity, albeit an irregular one. This periodicity is simply an indication of the underlying recurring instinctual tension.

Partly because of internal reasons and partly because of environmental exciting factors, every now and again a child becomes an excitable being. The phrase 'all dressed up and nowhere to go' might have been designed to describe this state. A study of what happens to this excitement is almost a study of childhood, and of the child's problem: how to retain the capacity for eagerness and excitement without experiencing too much painful frustration through lack of satisfactory climax. The main methods by which children cope with this difficulty are:

(a) Loss of capacity for eagerness; but this carries with it a loss of sense of body, and much else that is disadvantageous.

(b) Employment of some sort of reliable climax, either eating or drinking or masturbation, or excited urination or defecation, or a temper tantrum, or a fight.

(c) The perversion of the body functions in a way that enables a spurious climax to be reached – vomiting and diarrhoea, a bilious attack, exaggeration of a catarrhal infection, complaint of aches and pains that would otherwise be unnoticed.

(d) A general muddle of all these, with a period of unwellness, perhaps with headache and loss of appetite, a period of general irritability, or a tendency of certain tissues to be excitable (for instance, all the phenomena clumped together, in present-day nomenclature, under the word 'allergic').

(e) An organization of excitement into a chronic 'nerviness' which may remain constant over a long period ('common anxious restlessness', perhaps the most common disorder of childhood).

The bodily symptoms and changes related to emotional states and disorders of emotional development form a large and important subject for the attention of the paediatrician.

In a description of childhood sexuality, mention must be made of masturbation. Here again is a vast subject for study. Masturbation is either normal or healthy or else it is a symptom of a disorder of emotional development. Compulsive masturbation, just like compulsive thigh-rubbing, nail-biting, rocking, head-banging, head-swaying or rolling, thumb-sucking, and the like, is evidence of anxiety of one kind or another. If severely compulsive it is being employed by the child in his effort to deal with anxiety of more primitive or psychotic type, such as fear of disintegration of personality, or fear of loss of sense of the body, or fear of loss of touch with external reality.

Perhaps the most common disorder of masturbation is its suppression, or its disappearance from a child's repertoire of self-managed defences against intolerable anxiety or sense of deprivation or loss. An infant starts life with the capacity to handle his mouth and to suck his fist, and indeed he needs this ability to comfort himself. He needs his hand to his mouth even if he has what is best for him, a right to his mother's breast when he feels hungry. How much more does he need it when he is regimented. All through infancy he needs whatever satisfaction he can get from his body, from fist-sucking, from passing water, from defecation, and from holding his penis. The little girl has corresponding satisfactions.

Ordinary masturbation is no more than an employment of natural resources for satisfaction as an insurance against frustration and consequent anger, hate, and fear. Compulsive masturbation simply implies that the underlying anxieties to be dealt with are excessive. Perhaps the infant needs feeding at shorter intervals, or he needs more mothering; or he needs to be able to know that someone is always near at hand, or his mother is so anxious that she ought to allow him more quiet lying in a pram, and less contact with her. It is logical to try to deal with the underlying anxiety when masturbation is a symptom, but illogical to try to stop the masturbation. It must be recognized, however, that in rare cases compulsive masturbation is continuous and is so exhausting that it has to be stopped by repressive measures, simply in order to give the child some relief from his or her own symptom. When relief is obtained in this way new difficulties must appear in the child's adolescence, but the need for immediate relief can be so great that troubles a few years ahead seem relatively unimportant.

When all goes well, masturbation accompanying sexual ideas happens without being much noticed, or is only recognized through a child's breathing changes, or because of a sweating head. Trouble follows, however, when there is a combination of compulsion to masturbate with inhibition of sex feeling. In this case the child becomes exhausted by his efforts to produce the satisfaction and climax that he cannot easily attain. To give up involves a loss of sense of reality, or loss of the sense of value. To persist, however, leads eventually to physical debility, and the notorious rings under the eyes which indicate conflict, and which are commonly ascribed wrongly to masturbation itself. Sometimes it is kind to help a child out of this impasse by paternal strictness.

Psychoanalytic study of children (as of adults) shows that the male genital is valued much more highly in the unconscious than would appear from direct observation, although of course many children do express their interest in the penis openly, if they are allowed. Little boys value their genitalia just as they value their toes and other parts of their bodies, but in so far as they experience sexual excitement they know the penis has special importance. Erection associated with love feelings determines castration fears. The penis excitement of a boy infant has its fantasy parallel, and a great deal depends upon the type of fantasy that goes with the early erections.

The onset of genital excitement is variable. Genital excitement may be almost absent in early infancy or, alternatively, erections may be almost constantly present from birth. Naturally, no good can come from artificial awakening of penis excitement. It seems likely that the dressings after circumcision frequently stimulate erections and cause an unnecessary association of erection with pain, this being one of several reasons why circumcision should almost never be performed (except on religious grounds). It is convenient when genital excitement is not a marked feature before the other parts of the body have become established as having an importance of their own, and certainly any artificial stimulation of the genitals of infants (either by post-operative procedure or by the desire of uneducated nannies to produce soothing sleep) is a complication; and the process of the child's emotional development is complex enough inherently.

To the little girl the visible and palpable boy's genitalia (scrotum included) are very liable to become an object of envy, but especially in respect of her attachment to her mother developing along identification-with-man lines. However, the matter is not as simple as this, and no doubt a large proportion of little girls are quite contented to have their own more hidden but just as important genitalia, and to allow boys their more vulnerable male appendages. In time a girl learns to evaluate the breasts. These become almost as important to her as the penis is to the boy, and when a girl knows she has the capacity, which a boy has not, to carry and produce as well as to feed babies, she knows she has nothing to envy. Nevertheless, she must envy the boy if she is driven by anxiety back from ordinary heterosexual development to what is called a fixation to her mother, or a mother-figure, with a consequent need to be like a man. Naturally, if a little girl is not allowed or does not allow herself to know she has an exciting and important part of her body in her genitalia, or is not allowed to refer to it, her tendency to penis envy is increased.

Clitoris excitement is closely associated with urinary erotism, which lends itself more to the kind of fantasy that goes with identification with the male. Through clitoris erotism the girl knows what it would feel like to be a boy with penis erotism. Similarly, a boy can experience in the skin of the perineum feelings that correspond to those that belong to the vulva of a girl.

This is quite separate from the anal erotism which is normally a feature in either sex, and provides, along with oral, urethral, muscle, and skin erotism, an early root of sex.

There is no lack of evidence in sociology and folk lore and in the myths and legends of primitive peoples of the paternal or ancestral penis, worshipped in symbolic form and exerting immense influence. In the modern home these things are as important as ever, although they are hidden; but their importance appears when a child's home breaks up, and he suddenly loses the symbols on which he had come to rely, so that he is at sea without a compass, and he is in distress.

A child is so much more than sex. In the same way your favourite flower is so much more than water; yet a botanist would fail in his job if in describing a plant he forgot to mention water, of which it is chiefly composed. In psychology fifty years ago there really was a danger that the sex part of child life might have been left out because of the taboo on childhood sexuality.

The sexual instinct gathers together in childhood, in a highly complex way, out of all its components, and exists as something that enriches and complicates the whole life of the healthy child. Many of the fears of childhood are associated with sexual ideas and excitements, and with the consequent conscious and unconscious mental conflicts. Difficulties of the sexual life of the child account for many psychosomatic disorders, especially those of recurring type.

The basis for adolescent and adult sexuality is laid down in childhood, and also the roots of all sexual perversions and difficulties.

The prevention of adult sexual disorders, as well as the prevention of all but the purely hereditary aspects of mental and psychosomatic illness, is in the province of those who care for infants and children.

Chapter 24

Stealing and Telling Lies

The mother who has had several healthy children will know that each one of them presented acute problems every now and again, especially when two, three, and four years old. One child had a period of night-screaming of very severe intensity so that the neighbours thought that she was being ill-treated. Another one absolutely refused to be trained to be clean. Another one was so clean and good that the mother was worried lest the child should be completely lacking in spontaneity and personal enterprise. Yet another of her children was liable to terrific temper tantrums, perhaps with head banging and the holding of breath, until the mother was at her wit's end, and the child was blue in the face and as near to having a fit as possible. A long list could be made of this sort of thing happening naturally in the course of family life. One of these uncomfortable things that happen, and one that sometimes gives rise to special difficulties, is the habit of stealing.

Little children quite regularly take pennies out of their mothers' handbags. Usually there is no problem here whatever. The mother is quite tolerant of the way the child carries on, turning out the contents of her bag, and generally messing things up. She is rather amused, when she troubles to notice it. She may even have two bags, one of which the child never gets to at all, while another more workaday one is available for the little child's exploration. Gradually the child just grows out of this and nothing more is thought of it. The mother quite rightly feels that this is healthy and a part of the child's initial relation to herself, and so to people in general.

We can easily see why it is, however, that occasionally one finds a mother really worried when her little child takes things that belong to her, and hides them. She has had experience of the other extreme, the thieving older child. There is nothing more disturbing to the happiness of a household than the presence in it of an older child (or grown-up for that matter) who is liable to steal. Instead of the general trusting of everyone, and a free and easy way of leaving things all over the place, there has to be a specialized technique designed to protect important possessions such as money, chocolates, sugar, etc. In this case there is someone ill in the house. Many people get a very nasty feeling when they think of this. They feel uneasy when they are confronted with thieving just as they do when the word masturbation is mentioned. Apart from their having met with thieves, people may find themselves very definitely upset at the very thought of thieving, because of battles they themselves have fought over their own thieving tendencies in their own childhood. It is because of this uncomfortable feeling about out-and-out thieving that mothers sometimes worry unnecessarily about the quite normal tendency of little children to take things from their own mothers' possessions.

After a moment's thought, it will be seen that in an ordinary household, one in which there is no ill person who could be called a thief, actually quite a lot of stealing goes on; only it is not called stealing. A child goes into the larder and takes a bun or two, or helps himself to a lump of sugar out of the cupboard. In a good home no one calls the child who does this a thief. (Yet the same child in an institution may be punished and branded because of the rules that happen to obtain there.) It may be necessary for parents to make rules in order to keep the home a going concern. They may have to make a rule that whereas the children can always go and take bread, or perhaps a certain kind of cake, they may not take special cakes, and may not eat sugar from the store-cupboard. There is always a certain amount of to-and-fro about these things, and life in a household to some extent consists in the working out of the relation between the parents and the children in these and similar terms.

But a child who, say, regularly goes and steals apples, and quickly gives them away without himself enjoying them, is acting under a compulsion, and is ill. He can be called a thief. He will not know why he has done what he has done, and if pressed for a reason he will become a liar. The thing is, what is this boy doing? (Certainly the thief may be a girl, but it is clumsy to use both pronouns each time.) *The thief is not looking for the object that he takes. He is looking for a person. He is looking for his own mother, only he does not know this.* To the thief it is not the fountain pen from Woolworths, or the bicycle from the neighbour's railings, or the apple from the orchard, that can give satisfaction. A child who is ill in this way is incapable of enjoying the possession of things stolen. He is only acting out a fantasy which belongs to his primitive love impulses, and the best he can do is to enjoy the acting out, and the skill exercised. The fact is that he has lost touch with his mother in some sense or other. The mother may or may not still be there. She may even be there, and a perfectly good mother, and able to give him any amount of love. From the child's point of view, however, there is something missing. He may be fond of his mother and even in love with her, but, in a more primitive sense, for some reason or other she is lost to him. The child who is thieving is an infant looking for the mother, or for the person *from whom he has a right to steal*; in fact, he seeks the person from whom he can take things, just as, as an infant and a little child of one or two years old, he took things from his mother simply because she *was* his mother, and because he had rights over her.

There is one further point; *his own mother is really his, because he invented her.* The idea of her arose gradually out of his own capacity to love. We may know that Mrs So-and-so, who has had six children, at a certain time gave birth to this baby Johnny, and that she fed him and looked after him, and then eventually had another child. From Johnny's point of view, however, when he was born this woman was something he created; by actively adapting herself to his needs, she showed him what it would be sensible to create, as it was actually there. What his mother gave to him of herself had to be conceived of, had to be *subjective* for him before *objectivity* began to mean anything. Ultimately, in the tracing down of thieving to its roots, it can always be found that the thief has a need to re-establish his relation to the world on the basis of a re-finding of the person who, because she is devoted to him, understands him and is willing to make an active adaptation to his needs; in fact, to give him the illusion that the world contains what he can conceive of, and to enable him to place what he conjures up just where there actually is a devoted person in external 'shared' reality.

What is the practical application of this? The point is that the healthy infant in each one of us only gradually becomes able to perceive objectively the mother whom at first he created. This painful process is what is called disillusionment, and there is no need actively to disillusion a small child; rather can it be said that the ordinary good mother holds back disillusionment, and allows it only in so far as she feels the infant can take it, and welcome it.

A two-year-old child who is stealing pennies from mother's handbag is playing at being a hungry infant who thought he created his mother, and who assumed that he had rights over her and her contents. Disillusionment can come only too quickly. The birth of a new baby, for instance, can be a terrible shock just in this particular way even when the child is prepared for his or her advent and even when there is good feeling towards the new baby. The sudden access of disillusionment in respect of a little child's feeling that he created his own mother which the advent of the new baby can cause, easily starts a phase of compulsive stealing. Instead of playing at having full rights over his mother, the child may be found to be compulsively taking things, especially sweet things, and hiding them, but without really getting satisfaction from having them. If parents understand what this phase of a more compulsive type of stealing means they will act sensibly. They will tolerate it, for one thing, and they will try to see that the child whose nose has been put out of joint can at least rely on a certain quantity of special personal attention, at a certain time each day; and the time for starting the weekly penny may have arrived. Above all, parents who understand this situation will not come down like a ton of bricks on the child and demand confession. They will know that if they do so the child will certainly start lying as well as thieving, and it will be absolutely their fault.

These are common matters in ordinary healthy households, and in the vast majority of cases the whole thing is got through sensibly, and the child who is temporarily under compulsion to steal things recovers.

There is a vast difference, however, according to whether parents understand enough about what is happening to avoid unwise action, or whether they feel they must 'cure' the thieving in its early stages, in order to prevent the child from becoming a confirmed thief at a later date. Even when things eventually go well the amount of unnecessary suffering which children undergo through mismanagement of this sort of detail is tremendous. The essential suffering is sufficient indeed. It is not only in respect of thieving. In all sorts of ways children who have suffered some too great or sudden access of disillusionment find themselves under a compulsion to do things without knowing why, to make messes, to refuse to defecate at the correct moment, to cut the heads off the plants in the garden, etc.

Parents who feel they must get to the bottom of these acts, and who ask children to explain why they have done what they have done, are vastly increasing the children's difficulties, which are already intense enough just then. A child cannot give the real reason, not knowing it, and the result may be that, instead of feeling almost unbearable guilt as a result of being misunderstood and blamed, he will become split in his person; split into two parts, one terribly strict, and the other possessed by evil impulses. The child then no longer feels guilty, but is instead being transformed into what people will call a liar.

The shock of having one's bicycle stolen is not, however, mitigated by the knowledge that the thief was unconsciously looking for his mother. This is altogether another kettle of fish. Revenge feelings in the victim can certainly not be ignored, and any attempt to be sentimental about delinquent children defeats its own aim by raising the tension of general antagonism towards criminals. Magistrates in a juvenile court cannot only think of the thief as ill, and cannot ignore the anti-social nature of the delinquent act, and the irritation which this must engender in the localized bit of society which is affected. Indeed we are putting a tremendous strain on society when we ask the courts to recognize the fact that a thief is ill, so that treatment rather than punishment may be prescribed.

There is of course much stealing which never comes into the

courts, because it is dealt with satisfactorily in the home of the child by ordinary good parents. One can say that a mother feels no strain when her small child is stealing from her, as she would never dream of calling this stealing, and she easily recognizes that what the child is doing is an expression of love. In the management of the four- and five-year-old child, or the child who is passing through a phase in which there is a certain amount of compulsive stealing, there is of course some strain on the parents' tolerance. We should give these parents anything that we can give in the way of understanding of the processes involved, in order to help them to carry their own children through to social adjustment. It is for this reason that I have tried to put down one person's point of view, deliberately simplifying the problem in order to present it in a form that can be understood by the good parent or teacher.

Chapter 25

First Experiments in Independence

Psychology is liable to be superficial and easy, or else deep and difficult. A curious thing about the study of the first activities of infants, and the objects they use when going to sleep or when apprehensive, is that these things seem to exist in a layer in between the superficial and the deep, in between the simple examination of obvious facts and a probing into the obscure realms of the unconscious. For this reason I want to draw attention to the use infants make of ordinary common objects, and to show that there is a great deal to be learned from observations which are commonly made, and from facts which are all the time on display.

I am talking about nothing more difficult than the ordinary normal child's teddy bear. Everyone who has care of children has interesting details to give which are as characteristic in the case of each child as the other behaviour patterns, and which are never exactly the same in two cases.

At the beginning, as everyone knows, infants mostly push their fists into their mouths, and very soon they are developing a pattern, perhaps choosing a certain finger, two fingers, or a thumb, for sucking, while with the other hand caressing some part of the mother or a bit of sheet, blanket, or wool, or perhaps their own hair. There are two things going on here; the first, with some part of the hand in the mouth, being clearly related to the excited feeding; the second is one stage further displaced from excitement, and is more nearly affectionate. Out of this affectionate fondling activity there can develop a relationship to something which happens to be lying around, and this object may become very important to the infant. In a sense this is the first possession, that is, the first thing in the world that belongs to the infant, and yet which is not part of the infant like the thumb, or the two fingers, or the mouth. How important this can be, therefore, is evidence of the beginning of a relationship to the world.

These things develop along with the beginning of a sense of security, and along with the beginnings of the infant's relationship to one person. They are evidence that things are going well in the child's emotional development, and that memories of relationships are beginning to be built up. These can be made use of again in this new relationship to the object, which I myself like to call a transitional object. It is not the object itself, of course, that is transitional; it represents the infant's transition from a state of being merged with the mother to a state of being in relation to the mother as something outside and separate.

Although I want to stress the health that is implied in these phenomena, I do not want to give the impression that something is necessarily wrong if an infant does not develop interests of the kind that I am describing. In some cases the mother herself is retained and needed in person by an infant, whereas another infant finds this so-called transitional object good enough and even perfect, provided the mother is there in the background. It is common, however, for an infant to become specifically attached to some object which soon acquires a name, and it is fun to look into the origin of the name, which often derives from some word that the infant has heard long before speech has become possible. Soon, of course, parents and relations present the infant with soft playthings which (perhaps for the sake of the grown-ups) are shaped like animals or babies. From the infant's point of view these shapes are not so important. It is more the texture and the smell which take on vital significance, and the smell is especially important, so that parents learn that these objects cannot be washed with impunity. Parents who are otherwise hygienic often find themselves forced to carry around a filthy smelly soft object simply for peace. The infant, now growing up a little, needs this to be available; needs it to be returned when thrown away over and over again from the cot and the pram; needs to be able to pull bits out of it, and to dribble over it. In fact, there is nothing that may not happen to this thing, which becomes subjected to a very primitive form of loving – a mixture of affectionate caressing and destructive attack. In time other objects are added, and these are more and more appropriately fashioned to resemble animals or babies. Moreover, as time goes on, the parents try to get the child to say 'ta', which means to acknowledge the fact that the doll or the teddy bear came from the world, and was not born out of the imagination of the infant.

If we go back to the first object, which may perhaps be a Harrington square, or a special woollen scarf, or the mother's handkerchief, we must admit, I believe, that from the infant's point of view it would be inappropriate for us to ask for the word 'ta', and the acknowledgement of the fact that the object came from the world. From the infant's point of view this first object was indeed created out of his or her imagination. It was the beginning of the infant's creation of the world, and it seems that we have to admit that in the case of every infant the world has to be created anew. The world as it presents itself is of no meaning to the newly-developing human being unless it is created as well as discovered.

It is impossible to do justice to the enormous variety of the early possessions and techniques employed by infants at times of stress, and particularly at times of going to sleep.

A baby girl used her mother's rather long hair for caressing while thumb-sucking. When her own hair was long enough she pulled it – instead of her mother's – across her face, and sniffed at it, when she was going to sleep. She did this regularly until she was old enough to want to have her hair cut so as to be like a boy. She was pleased with the result until bedtime, when, of course, she became frantic. Fortunately, the parents had kept her hair, and a switch of it was given to her. Immediately she put it across her face in the ordinary way, sniffed at it, and went to sleep happily.

A baby boy became early interested in a coloured woollen covering. Before he was a year old he had become interested in sorting out the threads of wool that he had pulled out according to their colours. His interest in the texture of wool and in colours persisted, and in fact never left him, so that when he grew up he became a colour expert in a textile factory.

The values of the examples can only be that they illustrate the wide range of the phenomena and of the techniques employed by infants in health, at moments of stress and separation. Almost anyone caring for children can supply examples, each one of which is fascinating to study, provided one first of all realizes that every detail is important and significant. Sometimes, instead of objects we find techniques, like humming, or more hidden activities such as the matching of lights seen, or the study of the interplay of borders – as between two curtains that move slightly in the breeze, or the overlap of two objects that change in relation to each other according to movements of the infant's head. Sometimes thinking takes the place of visible activities.

In order to stress the normality of these matters I would like to draw attention to the way in which separation can affect them. Roughly speaking, when the mother, or some other person on whom the infant is dependent, is absent, there is no immediate change, owing to the fact that the infant has an internal version of the mother which remains alive for a certain length of time. If the mother is away over a period of time which is beyond a certain limit, then the internal version fades; at the same time all these transitional phenomena become meaningless, and the infant is unable to make use of them. What we see now is an infant who must be nursed or fed, and who if left alone, tends to go over into exciting activities with sensuous gratification. What is lost is the whole intermediate area of affectionate contact. With the return of the mother, if the interval has not been too long, there first builds up a new internal version of her, and this takes time. The success of this re-establishment of confidence in the mother is shown by the return of the employment of intermediate activities. What we see in infants becomes more obviously serious when at a later stage a child feels abandoned, and becomes unable to play, and unable to be affectionate or to accept affection. Along with this, as is well known, there can be compulsive erotic activities. The stealing of deprived children who are recovering can be said to be part of the search for the transitional object, which had been lost through the death or fading of the internalized version of the mother.

A baby girl always sucked a rough woollen cloth wrapped round her thumb. At three she was 'cured' of thumb-sucking by having the rag taken away. Later she developed a very severe compulsive nail-biting which accompanied compulsive reading at the time of going to sleep.

The nail-biting ceased when, at eleven years, she was helped to remember the woollen cloth, the pattern on it, and her love of it.

In health there is an evolution from the transitional phenomenon, and the use of objects, to the whole play capacity of the child. It is very easy to see that playing is of vital importance to all children, and that the capacity for play is a sign of health in emotional development. I am trying to draw attention to the fact that an early version of this is the relationship of the infant to the first object. My hope is that if parents understand that these transitional objects are normal, and indeed signs of healthy growth, they will not feel ashamed when they find themselves carrying curious things about with them whenever they travel with their child. They will certainly not show disrespect for them, and they will do everything possible to avoid their loss. Like old soldiers these objects simply fade away. In other words they become the group of phenomena extending out into the whole of the realm of children's play, and of cultural activities and interests – that wide area which is intermediate between living in the external world and dreaming.

Evidently the task of sorting out external phenomena from dreams is a heavy one. It is a task that we all hope to be able to accomplish, so that we may claim to be sane. Nevertheless, we need a resting-place from this sorting-out, and we get it in our cultural interests and activities. For the little child we allow a wider area than we allow for ourselves in which imagination plays a dominant role, so that playing which makes use of the world, and yet retains all the intensity of the dream, is considered characteristic of the life of children. For the infant who is just starting on this terrible task of achieving adult sanity we allow an intermediate life, particularly at the time between waking and sleeping, and these phenomena that I am referring to, and the objects which are used, belong to the resting-place that we give to the infant at the beginning, when we only very slightly expect the sorting out of the dream from the real.

As a child psychiatrist, when I get into contact with children and find them drawing pictures, and talking about themselves and their dreams, I find to my surprise that children easily remember these very early objects. Often they surprise their parents by remembering bits of cloth and weird objects which the parents had long forgotten. If an object is still available, it is the child who knows just where, in the limbo of half-forgotten things, this thing still lies, perhaps right at the back of a bottom drawer, or up on the top shelf of a cupboard. It is distressing for children not only when the object is lost, as happens sometimes by accident, but also when some parent with a lack of understanding of its real significance gives it away to another baby. Some parents are so used to the idea of these objects that, as soon as a baby is born, they take the transitional object of the family, and tuck it up with the baby, expecting that it will have the same effect on the new baby as it had on the last one. Naturally, they may be disappointed, because the object turning up in this way may or may not come to have significance for the new infant. It all depends. It can readily be seen that to present an object in this way has its dangers, since, in a sense, it robs the new infant of the opportunity for creating. Certainly it is often very helpful when a child can make use of some object in the home; something that can be given a name, and that often becomes almost part of the family. Out of the infant's interest in this comes his eventual preoccupation with dolls, other toys, and animals.

This whole subject is a fascinating one for parents to study. They need not be psychologists in order to get a great deal of profit from watching, and perhaps recording, a line of development of such attachments and techniques in this intermediate area characteristic of each of their infants in turn.

Chapter 26

Support for Normal Parents

If you have read as far as this you will have seen that I have tried to say something positive. I have not shown how difficulties can be overcome, or what ought to be done when children show signs of anxiety, or when parents quarrel in front of their children, but I have tried to give a little support to the sound instincts of normal parents, those who are likely to achieve and maintain a family of ordinary healthy children. There is much more to be said, but here is my attempt at a start.

It may be asked: Why trouble to talk to people who are doing well; surely the greater need comes from those parents who are in difficulties? Well, I try not to be weighed down by the fact that much distress undoubtedly exists even here in England, in London, in the district immediately around the hospital where I work. I know only too well about this distress, and about the anxiety and depression that prevail. But my hopes are based on the stable and healthy families which I also see building up around me, families that form the only basis for the stability of our society for the next couple of decades.

It may also be asked: Why concern yourself with healthy families which you say exist, and on which you base your hopes? Can they not manage for themselves? Well, I have a very good reason for giving active support here, which is this: there exist tendencies towards destruction of these good things. It is by no means wise to assume that what is good is safe from attack; rather is it true to say that the best always has to be defended if it is to survive discovery. There is always hate of what is good, and fear of it, chiefly unconscious, liable to appear in the form of interferences, petty regulations, legal restrictions, and all manner of stupidities.

I do not mean that parents are ordered about or cramped by

official policy. The State in England takes pains to leave parents free to choose, and to accept or refuse what the State offers. Of course, births and deaths have to be registered, certain infectious diseases are notifiable, and children must attend school from five to fifteen. And boys and girls who break the law of the land come, with their parents, under some form of compulsion. However, the State provides a very large number of services which parents may make use of or may eschew. To mention a few, there are the nursery schools, vaccination against smallpox, immunization against diphtheria, ante-natal and infant welfare clinics, cod-liver oil and fruit juices, dental treatment, cheap milk for infants and school milk for the older children; all these are available yet not compulsory. All of which suggests that the State in England today does recognize the fact that a good mother is the right judge of what is good for her own child, provided she is informed as to facts and educated as to needs.

The trouble is, as has already been suggested, that those who actually administer these public services are by no means uniformly confident in the mother's ability to understand her child better than anyone else can. Doctors and nurses are often so impressed with the ignorance and stupidity of some of the parents that they fail to allow for the wisdom of the others. Or perhaps the lack of confidence in mothers that is so often to be noted arises out of the specialized training of the doctors and nurses, who have expert knowledge of the body in sickness and in health, but who are not necessarily qualified to understand the parents' whole task. How easy for them to think, when a mother questions their expert advice, that she is doing so out of cussedness, when really she knows that it would harm her baby to be taken away from her to hospital at the time he is being weaned, or that her boy ought to be able to understand more of what the world is like before he is whisked into hospital for circumcision, or that her girl is actually the wrong type for injections and immunizations (unless there is actually an epidemic) because of extreme nervousness.

What is a mother to do if she is worried by the doctor's decision that her child's tonsils should be removed? The doctor certainly knows about tonsils, but often he fails to impress the mother that he really understands how serious it is to take a child who feels well at the time and to operate on him when he is too young to have the matter explained to him. The mother can only stick up for her belief in the necessity of avoiding such an event if possible, and if she really believes in her instinct because she is educated in this matter of her child's developing personality, she can put her point of view to the doctor and play her part in coming to a decision. A doctor who respects the specialized knowledge of the parent easily wins respect for his own specialized knowledge.

Parents know that their own little children need to be provided with a simplified environment, and that they need this simplified environment until they are able to understand the significance of complications, and are therefore able to allow for these. There comes a time when the son and heir can have his tonsils out, if they really need removal, without harm to his personality development, and he may even find interest and pleasure in his hospital experience, and make a step forward through having been over the top, so to speak. But this time depends on the kind of child the boy is, not only on his age; and only one as intimate with him as his mother is can judge, though to be sure a doctor ought to be able to help her think it all out.

The State is indeed wise in its policy of education of parents with non-compulsion, and the next step is education of those who administer the public services, and the deepening of their respect for the ordinary mother's feelings and instinctual knowledge regarding her own children. She is a specialist in this matter of her own children, and, if she is not over-awed by the voice of authority, she can be found to know well what is good and what is bad in the matter of management.

Whatever does not specifically back up the idea that parents are responsible people will in the long run be harmful to the very core of society.

What is significant is the individual's experience of developing from an infant into a child and an adolescent, in a family that continues to exist, and that considers itself capable of coping with its own localized problems – the problems of the world in miniature. In miniature, yes . . . but not smaller in regard to intensity of feelings and richness of experience, smaller only in the relatively unimportant sense of quantity of complexity.

If my writing does no more than stimulate others to do better what I am doing here, to support ordinary people, and to give them the real and right reasons for their good intuitive feelings, then I shall be satisfied. Let us do all we can as doctors and nurses for the sick both in body and mind, and let the State do all it can for those who for one reason or another are left stranded, and need care and protection. But let us also remember that there are, fortunately, some normal men and women, especially among the less sophisticated members of the community, who are not afraid of feelings, and whose feelings we need not fear. To bring out the best in parents, we must leave them full responsibility with regard to what is their own affair, the upbringing of their own family.

Part Three

The Outside World

Chapter 27

Needs of the Under-Fives

The needs of infants and small children are not variable; they are inherent and unalterable.

It is necessary to think all the time of the developing child. This is always a helpful approach, but it is especially important in the case of the under-fives, since each child of four is also three and also two and also one, and is also an infant being weaned, or an infant just born, or even an infant in the womb. Children go backwards and forwards in their emotional age.

It is a long distance from the new-born babe to the five-year-old child in terms of personality and emotional growth. This distance cannot be covered except by the provision of certain conditions. These conditions need only be good enough, since a child's intelligence becomes increasingly able to allow for failures and to deal with frustrations by advance preparation. As is well known, the conditions that are necessary for the child's individual growth are themselves not static, set, and fixed, but are in a state of qualitative and quantitative change relative to the infant's or the child's age and changing needs.

Consider closely the healthy boy or girl of four. In the course of the day there can appear a degree of worldliness like that of an adult. The boy has become able to identify with father and the girl with mother, and there are also the cross-identifications. This capacity for identification shows in actual behaviour, and in the taking of responsibility for a limited time over a limited area; it shows in play in which the tasks and joys of married life, of parenthood, and of pedagogy are plainly displayed; it shows in the violent loves and jealousies which are characteristic of the age; and it exists in the day fantasies and especially and fundamentally in the dreams of the child asleep.

These are some of the mature elements in the healthy four-year-old, especially taking into consideration the intensity of living that derives from the child's instinct, the biological basis for excitements that show the sequence; preparation with increasing tension, climax, and then a measure of relaxation following some form of gratification.

In the full-blooded dream that marks the maturity that belongs to the period just before five, the child is at one apex of a triangle in human relationships. In this full-blooded dream the biological drive which we call instinct is accepted, and it is no mean feat for an individual child to keep up with biological growth, so that in the dream, and in the potential fantasy behind waking life, the child's bodily functions are involved in relationships of intense kind, with love felt as such, and also hate, and also the inherent conflicts.

This means that the whole range of sexuality is within the scope of the healthy child, except that there is the physical limitation belonging to physical immaturity. In symbolic form and in dream and in play the details of sexual relationships belong to childhood experience.

A need of the well-developed four-year-old is to have parents with whom to identify. At this important age it is no good implanting morals and inculcating cultural patterns. The operative factor is the parent, and the parent's behaviour, and the two parents' inter-relationship as perceived by the child. It is this that the child takes in, and imitates or reacts against, and it is this also that the child uses in a hundred ways in the personal process of self-development.

Moreover, the home, which has as its basis the relationship between the parents, has a function to perform by existing and by surviving; the child's expressed hate, and the hate that appears in the disasters of dreams, can be tolerated by the child because of the fact that the home continues to function in spite of the worst and because of the best.

But a child who is at times amazingly mature at four and a half suddenly becomes a two-year-old when in need of reassurance because of a cut finger or a chance fall, and is liable to become quite infantile at the time of going off to sleep. A child of any age who needs to be held affectionately needs a physical form of loving which was naturally given by the mother when she carried her infant in her womb and in her arms.

Indeed, the infant does not start off as a person able to identify with other people. There has had to be a gradual building up of the self as a whole or a unit, and there has to be a gradual development of the capacity to feel that the world outside and also the world within are related things, but not the same as the self, the self that is individual and peculiar and never the same in two children.

The attainment of a maturity appropriate to the age between three and five is emphasized first, because healthy infants and children are all the time building up for this maturity that is so vital to the whole future development of the individual. At the same time the maturity of the under-five child is normally compatible with every kind and degree of immaturity. The immaturities are the residues of the healthy states of dependence that are characteristic of all the earlier phases of growth. It is simpler to give soundings taken at the various phases of development than to attempt to paint the composite picture of the child of four.

Even in a condensed statement one must separate out the following elements:

(1) Triangular relationship (held by the family).

(2) Two-person relationship (mother introducing the world to the baby).

(3) Mother holding infant in unintegrated state (seeing the whole person before the infant feels whole).

(4) Mother's love expressed in terms of physical management (maternal techniques).

(1) *Triangular Relationship*. The child has become a whole human being among whole human beings, caught up in triangular relationships. In the underlying or unconscious dream the child is in love with one parent and in consequence hates the other. To some extent the hate is expressed in direct form, and that child is lucky who can gather together all the latent aggressive residue from the earlier phases to use in this hating, which is acceptable because its basis is primitive love. To some extent, however, this hate is absorbed in the child's ability to identify with the rival in the dream. Here the

family situation carries the child and the child's dream. The triangle has a reality form and this remains intact. The triangle is found also in all kinds of near relationships which allow a spreading out from the central theme and a gradual lessening of the tensions till they become just manageable in some real situation. Play is especially important here, since it is both real and also a dream, and although play experiences allow tremendous feelings of all kinds which otherwise stay locked up in the unremembered dream, the game eventually ceases, and those who are playing pack up and eat tea together, or prepare for bath and the bed-time story. Moreover, in play (at the period we are considering) there is always a grown-up person nearby who is indirectly involved, and who is ready to assume control.

A study of the two childhood games, fathers and mothers, and doctors and nurses, could easily be instructive to the new-comer to this subject, as well as the specific games based on the imitation of mother's work in the home and father's special job. Study of children's dreams demands special skill, but naturally takes the student further into the unconscious than the simple observation of children's play.

(2) *Two-person Relationship*. At an earlier stage, instead of the triangular relationship we get the more direct relationship between infant or small child and mother. In extremely subtle ways the mother is introducing the world to the baby, to a limited extent, by warding off chance impingements, and by supplying what is needed more or less in the right way and at the right time. It can easily be seen that in this two-body relationship there is much less room than in the triangular pattern for the individual child's personal management of awkward moments; in other words there is greater dependence. Nevertheless there are two whole human beings, intimately inter-related, and interdependent. If the mother is herself healthy, not anxious, depressive, muddled, or with-drawn, then there is a wide scope for the growth of the small child's personality in the day-to-day enrichment of the infant–mother relationship.

(3) *Mother Holding Infant in Unintegrated State*. Earlier than this there is, of course, an even greater degree of dependence. The mother is needed as someone who survives each day, and

who can integrate the various feelings, sensations, excitements, angers, griefs, etc. that go to make up an infant's life but which the infant cannot hold. The infant is not yet a unit. The mother is holding the infant, the human being in the making. The mother can, if necessary, go over in her mind all that the day has meant to the infant. She understands. She sees her infant as human at a time when the infant is incapable of feeling integrated.

(4) *Mother's Love Expressed in Terms of Physical Management*. Still earlier the mother is holding her infant, and this time I mean it physically. All the very early details of *physical* care are *psychological* matters for the infant. The mother makes an active adaptation to the infant's needs, and at the start this adaptation can be remarkably complete. The mother knows, instinctively as people say, what need is just about to become pressing. She presents the world to the infant in the only way that does not spell chaos, by the meeting of needs as they arise. Also by expressing love in terms of physical management and in the giving of physical satisfactions she enables the infant psyche to begin to live in the infant body. By her technique of infant care she expresses her feeling towards her infant, and builds herself up as a person who can be recognized by the developing individual.

This statement of needs is given as a basis for a discussion of the impact on the child of the various changes which have been observed in the family pattern. Such needs each in their own way are absolute, taking into account their changing quality. Failure to meet such needs results in a distortion of the individual child's development, and it can be taken as an axiom that the more primitive the type of need the greater is the dependence of the individual on the environment, and the more disastrous the failure to meet such needs. The early management of an infant is a matter beyond conscious thought and deliberate intention. It is something that becomes possible only through *love*. We sometimes say the infant needs love, but we mean that only someone who loves the infant can make the necessary adaptation to need, and only someone who loves the infant can graduate a failure of adaptation to follow the growth of the individual child's capacity and make positive use of failure.

The essential needs of the under-fives belong to the individuals concerned, and the basic principles do not change. This truth is applicable to human beings of the past, present, and future, anywhere in the world, and in any culture.

Parents and Their Sense of Job

There seems to be in young parents today a new sense of doing a job; this is one of those many important things that do not appear in statistical inquiry. Modern parents wait; they plan, and they read. They know they will be able to give proper attention only to two or three children, and so they set out to do their limited parental job in the best possible way: they do it themselves. The result, when all goes well, is a directness of relationship which is itself alarming in its intensity and richness. We expect, and find, special difficulties arising out of the lack of displacements on to nurses and minders. The triangle of parents and child becomes a reality indeed.

It can be seen that parents who are so deliberately set on a job, that of starting their children off well on the road to mental health, are themselves individualists. It is part and parcel of this individualism that the parents themselves may later need to make further personal growth. In modern society there is a lessening of sham.

These parents who feel they are on a job provide a rich setting for the infant and small child. Moreover, if real help is available such parents make use of it. But this help must be of such a kind that it does not undermine the parents' sense of responsibility.

The birth of a new baby can be a valuable experience for the older child, or can be a great trouble, and parents who are willing to give time for consideration are able to avoid avoidable errors. However, it must not be expected that by taking thought we can prevent love, hate, and conflict of loyalties. Life is difficult and for no one more difficult than for the normal healthy child of three to five. Fortunately life is rewarding also, and at this early age it holds out promise, provided the home feels stable, and the child gets the sensation of happiness and contentment in the parents' inter-relationship.

Parents who set out to be adequate parents certainly give

themselves a big task, and there is always the risk that there will be no reward. Many chance circumstances may rob the parents of success, but fortunately there is much less risk from physical illness than there was twenty years ago. Parents are willing to study the needs of their children, and this helps; it must be remembered, however, that if things go wrong between them, parents cannot love each other just because the children need them to be in stable relationship.

Society and Its Sense of Responsibility

There has been a vast change in society's attitude towards infant and child care. There is now the understanding that in infancy and childhood is laid the basis for mental health, and eventually for maturity in terms of the adult who can identify with society without loss of sense of self-importance.

The great advances of paediatrics in the first half of this century have been mainly on the physical side. The idea has grown up that if physical disease in a child can be prevented or cured the psychology of the child can be left to take care of itself. Paediatrics still needs to rise above this basic principle, and will have to find a way of doing so without losing grip on the care of physical health. The work of Dr John Bowlby, who has concentrated on one thing, the ill effect on a small child of separation from the mother, has produced a very big change in procedure in the last few years, so that mothers now visit their children in hospital, and wherever possible a separation is avoided. Moreover, there has been a change of policy in the management of deprived children, with a virtual abolition of the residential nursery and an increasing development of the use of the foster-home. But the paediatricians and nurses who cooperate in these matters are still lacking in true understanding of the reasons behind the small child's need for continuity of relationship with the mother and father. It is an important step forward, however, if it is recognized that much mental ill-health can be prevented by the avoidance of unnecessary separations. What is still needed is a better understanding of the building up of the child's mental health in the normal family setting.

Again, doctors and nurses know a great deal about the physical side of pregnancy and childbirth, and about the infant's bodily health in the first months of life. They do not know, however, about the bringing together of a mother and baby in the first feeds, because this is a delicate matter which is beyond rules and regulations, and only the mother herself can know how to do this. Very great distress is caused universally by interference by experts in other skills, just when the mother is finding her way with her baby at the start.

We need to see that the trained worker in the field (maternity nurse, health visitor, nursery-school teacher, etc., each a specialist in a job) may be an immature personality compared with a father or mother, and the parents *judgement* over a specific matter may be more sound that that of the worker. This need cause no difficulty if the point is understood. The trained worker is necessary because of his or her special knowledge and skill.

What parents need all along is enlightenment about underlying causes, not advice, and not instruction as to procedure. Parents must also be given room for experiment and for making mistakes, so that they can learn.

The spread of social case work into the psychological field, which can immediately prove its value on the preventive side through the acceptance of broad principles of management, nevertheless provides a great threat to the normal or healthy family life. It is wise to remember that the health of the country depends on healthy family units with parents who are emotionally mature individuals. These healthy families are therefore sacred territory, not to be entered except with real understanding of positive values. Nevertheless, the healthy family unit needs help from wider units. The parents are all the time engaged in their own personal inter-relationship, and they are dependent on society for their own happiness and social integration.

Relative Lack of Siblings

A significant change in the family pattern is the relative lack not only of brothers and sisters but also of cousins. Do not let us imagine that we can supply cousins by supplying playmates. Blood relationship is of extreme importance in the gradual displacement of the child's two-body and three-body relationships outwards from the mother, and the father and mother to society in its wider aspect. It is to be expected that the modern child often has no help of the kind which was provided in the days of the large families. It must be common for a child to have no accessible cousin, and in the case of an only child this is a serious matter. Nevertheless, if this principle is accepted, we may say that the main help that can be given to the modern small family is in the extension of the range of relationship and opportunity. The nursery school, the nursery class, and the day nursery can do much, if not too big and if properly staffed. I refer not only to adequate staffing, but also to the education of staff in matters of infant and child psychology. Parents can use the nursery to give themselves a break; to enlarge the range of the infant's relationships both with adults and with other small children, and to enlarge the scope of playing.

Many normal or near-normal parents are irritable with their children if they have them all day and night, but if they have some hours to themselves they can be good with their child the rest of the time. I draw especial attention to this point, because in my practice I am always being confronted with the need for mothers to be helped when they seek part-time employment for the sake of their own health and equanimity. There is much room for argument here, but with regard to the healthy family (and I hope it will be accepted that this is not a rare phenomenon) the parents can take part in making variable decisions about nursery-school or day-nursery attendance.

In Great Britain education adapted to the nursery school has reached a very high standard. Our nursery schools have led the way in the world, partly through the influence of Margaret McMillan and my late friend Susan Isaacs. Moreover, the education of teachers for nursery-school work has affected the whole attitude towards teaching at later age groupings. It would be tragic indeed to see anything but further development of the sort of nursery school that is really suitable for giving help to the healthy family. By contrast, the day nursery is not primarily designed for the infant, and the authorities that support it are not certain to be properly interested in staffing or equipment. The day nursery is more likely than the nursery school to be under the dominance of the medical authorities who, I am sorry to say, since I am a doctor, sometimes seem to think that bodily growth and freedom from physical disease is all that matters. Nevertheless the day nursery can do some of the work which a really good nursery school, properly staffed and equipped, is designed to do and, above all, can enable tired and worried mothers to be good enough mothers because they have had a change of occupation.

Day nurseries will continue to find official support because of their more obvious value to society in distress; let them be well equipped and staffed else they must do harm to the normal children of healthy families. The nursery school at its best is so good that the good family in modern times can use it for sensible extensions of the scope of otherwise lonely small children; and because the good nursery school caters for the healthy family it has a very special, though intangible, non-statistical value to the community. Society must have a future if the present is to be taken seriously, and out of the healthy family comes the future.

Chapter 28

Mother, Teacher, and the Child's Needs*

The function of the nursery school is not to be a substitute for an absent mother, but to supplement and extend the role which in the child's earliest years the mother alone plays. The nursery school is probably most correctly considered as an extension 'upwards' of the family, rather than an extension 'downwards' of the primary school. It seems desirable, therefore, before discussing in any detail the role of the nursery school and of the teacher in particular, to set down a summary of what the infant needs from the mother, and the nature of the role that the mother plays in fostering healthy psychological development in the child's earliest years. It is only in the light of the mother's role and the child's needs that a real understanding can be gained of the way in which the nursery school can continue the mother's work.

Any statement of a child's need in infancy and at the nursery-school age must, if it is to be brief, do gross injustice to its subject. Nevertheless, even though a fully agreed and yet detailed statement could hardly be expected at the present stage of our knowledge, the account of broad outlines that follows appears to those members of the expert group particularly concerned with the clinical study of psychological development in infancy to be one that would be generally accepted by other workers in the field.

A few preliminary remarks are necessary on the respective roles of the mother, the nursery-school teacher, and the teacher of older children.

A *mother* need not have intellectual understanding of her job because she is fitted for it in its essentials by her biological orientation to her own baby. It is the fact of her devotion to

* Extracted from a UNESCO report. The author was one of the team of experts who built up the report, and this chapter is therefore not entirely his work.

her own baby rather than her self-conscious knowledge that makes her good enough to be successful in the early stages of infant nurture.

A *young nursery-school teacher* is not orientated biologically to any one child, except indirectly through identification with a mother figure. It is necessary therefore for her to be brought gradually to see that there exists a complex psychology of infant growth and adaptation, with need for special environmental conditions. Discussion of the children in her care will enable her to recognize the dynamic nature of normal emotional growth.

A *senior teacher* must be more able to appreciate intellectually the nature of this problem of growth and adaptation. Fortunately, she need not know everything, but she should be temperamentally fitted to accept the dynamic nature of growth processes and the complexity of the subject, and eager to increase her knowledge of detail by objective observations and by planned studies. She can be greatly helped by having opportunity for discussion of *theory* with child psychologists, psychiatrists, and psychoanalysts, and, of course, by reading.

The role of the father is vitally important, at first through his material and emotional support of his wife, and then gradually through his direct relation to his infant. At the nursery-school age, he may have become more important to his child than the mother. Nevertheless, it is not possible to do justice to the role of the father in the statement that follows.

The nursery-school years are significant because of the fact that a child at this period is in transition from one stage to another. While in some important ways and at some moments the two- to five-year-old child reaches to a maturity resembling that of the adolescent, in other ways and at other moments the same child is also (normally) immature and infantile. It is only when the mother's early care has been successful and when, in addition, the parents continue to provide the environmental essentials that the nursery-school teachers can give their mothering function second place to pre-school education proper.

In practice, every child at a nursery school is at certain moments and in certain ways an infant needing mothering (and fathering). Also to a greater or lesser extent there may have been maternal failure, and the nursery school then has the chance to supplement and correct maternal failure when this is not severe. For these reasons the young teacher needs to learn about mothering, and she has opportunity for this through her conversations with and through her observations of the mothers of the children in her care.

Normal Psychology of Childhood and Early Infancy

In the age period two to five or seven, each normal infant is experiencing the most intense conflicts which result from the powerful instinctual trends that enrich feelings and personal relationships. The quality of instinct has become less like that of early infancy (mainly alimentary) and more like that which is recognized later, at puberty, as the foundation of the sexual life of adults. The conscious and unconscious fantasy life of the child has taken on a new quality which makes possible identifications with mothers and fathers, wives and husbands, and the bodily accompaniments of these fantasy experiences have come to involve excitements which are like those of normal adults.

At the same time, relationships have only just become established as between whole human beings. Further, at this age, the little boy or girl is still learning to perceive external reality, and to understand that the mother has a life of her own, and that she cannot actually be possessed as she belongs to someone else.

The consequence of these developments is that ideas of love are followed by ideas of hate, by jealousy and painful emotional conflict, and by personal suffering; and where conflict is too great there follows loss of full capacity, inhibitions, 'repression',* etc., resulting in symptom formation. Expression of feeling is partly direct, but it is more and more possible, as the development of a child proceeds, for relief to be obtained by self-expression through play and through the medium of speech.

In these matters the nursery school has obvious important functions. One such is the provision for a few hours a day of an emotional atmosphere that is not the highly-charged one of

* This word is used in its technical psychological sense.

the home. This gives the child breathing-space for personal development. Also new triangular relationships less highly charged than at home can be formed and can be expressed among the children themselves.

The school, which stands for the home, but which is not an alternative to the child's home, can provide opportunity for a deep personal relationship with someone other than the child's parents. It provides this opportunity in the persons of the staff and the other children, and a generally tolerant but steady framework in which experiences can be lived through.

It is vital to remember, however, that at the same time that there are these evidences of achievement in the process of maturation, in other respects there is immaturity. For instance, the capacity for accurate perception is not fully developed, so that we expect from a small child a subjective rather than an objective conception of the world, especially at times such as those of going to sleep and waking. When anxiety threatens, the child easily returns to the infantile position of dependence, often with the consequence that infantile incontinence re-appears, as well as infantile intolerance of frustration. Because of this immaturity the school has to be able to take over the function of the mother who gave the infant confidence at the beginning.

It cannot be assumed that the child of nursery-school age has a fully established capacity to maintain love and hate of the same person. The more primitive way out of conflict is to split the good from the bad. The child's mother, who has inevitably stimulated in the child both love and anger, has continued to exist and to be herself, and by this she has enabled the child to begin to bring together what seems good and what seems bad in her; so the child has started to have guilt feelings, and to be concerned about the aggression that becomes directed towards her through love of her, and through her insufficiencies.

There is a time factor involved in the development of guilt and concern. The sequence is: love (with aggressive elements), hate, a period of digestion, guilt, reparation through direct expression or through constructive play. If the opportunity for reparation is missing, then the child must react by loss of capacity for guilt feeling, and ultimately by loss of capacity to love. The nursery school continues this work of the mother by the stability of its personnel, and also by its provision for constructive play, which enables each child to discover a way of dealing with the guilt that belongs to aggressive and destructive impulses.

A very important task already performed by the mother can be described under the term 'weaning'. Weaning implies that the mother has given something good, that she has waited till signs developed that the child was ready to be weaned, and that she has carried through with the task, in spite of arousing angry responses. When the child goes from home-care to school-care this experience is to some extent reproduced, so that a study of the weaning history of a child materially helps the young teacher to understand the initial difficulties which may appear at school. When a child takes to school easily the teacher can see this as an extension of the mother's success with her task of weaning.

There are other ways in which the mother, without knowing it, performs essential tasks in the laying down of the basis for her child's subsequent mental health. For instance, without her careful presentation of external reality the child has no means of making a satisfactory relationship with the world.

In nursery-school education, provision is made for that which is intermediate between the dream and the real; notably, play is respected in a positive way, and stories and drawings and music are employed. It is especially in this field that the nursery school can give enrichment and can help the child to find a working relationship between ideas that are free and behaviour that needs to become group-related.

By constantly looking for and seeing the human being in her infant, the mother has been enabling the infant gradually to come together as a personality, to integrate from within into a unit. This process is not completed by nursery-school age, and during this period the need continues for a personal type of relationship, with each child known by name, and dressed and treated according to what that child is and feels like. In the favourable case, the individuality of the child becomes in the course of time so firm that it is the child who wants to join in group activities.

The *physical* care of the infant from birth (or before) onwards has been a *psychological* process from the child's point of view.

The mother's technique of holding, of bathing, of feeding, everything she did to the baby, added up to the child's first idea of the mother, and to this there was gradually added her looks and her other physical attributes and her feelings.

The child's ability to feel that the body is the place where the psyche lives could not have developed without a consistent technique of handling, and when the nursery school continues with the provision of a physical environment and with the bodily care of the children, it is performing a main task of *mental* hygiene. Feeding is never simply a matter of getting food in; it is another way in which the school teacher continues the work of the mother. The school, like the mother, shows love by feeding the child, and, like the mother, expects to be refused (hated, suspected) as well as accepted (trusted). In the nursery school there is no place for what is impersonal or mechanical, because, for the child, this means hostility or (worse still) indifference.

The picture of the mother's role and the child's needs set out in this section makes it clear that the nursery-school teacher needs to be in touch with maternal functions, and this is consistent with the fact that her main task concerns the educational functions of the primary school. There is a lack of teachers of psychology, but everywhere there is a source of information which can be tapped by the nursery-school teacher if she be so directed: the observation of infant care by mothers and fathers, in the family setting.

The Role of the Nursery-school Teacher

On the assumption that the nursery school supplements and extends in certain directions the function of the good home, the nursery-school teacher naturally takes over some of the attributes and duties of the mother for the school period, without however seeking out of her own needs to develop a maternal emotional bond. Her duty is rather to maintain, strengthen, and enrich the child's personal relationship with the family, at the same time introducing a wider world of people and opportunities. Thus, from the time of the child's first entry into school a sincere and cordial relationship between the teacher and the mother will serve to arouse a sense of confidence in the mother and reassurance in the child. The establishment of such a relationship will help the teacher to detect and understand those disturbances in her children that arise from circumstances in the home, and in many cases it will afford opportunities to the teacher for helping mothers to have greater faith in themselves as mothers.

The entry into a nursery school is a social experience outside the family. It creates a psychological problem for the child and an opportunity for the nursery teacher to make her first mental-hygiene contribution.

The entry into the school may also create anxieties for the mother, who may misinterpret the child's need for the opportunities for development beyond the scope of the home, and who may feel that this need arises from her own inadequacy rather than from the child's natural development.

These problems, which arise on the child's entry into the nursery school, exemplify the fact that throughout the whole period at the nursery school the teacher has a dual responsibility, and a dual opportunity. She has the opportunity of assisting the mother to discover her own maternal potentialities, and of assisting the child in working through the inevitable psychological problems which face the developing human being.

Loyalty to the home and respect for the family are fundamental in the maintenance of firm relationships between the child, the teacher, and the family.

The teacher assumes the role of a warm-hearted and sympathetic friend, who will not only be the mainstay of the children's life away from home but also a person resolute and consistent in her behaviour towards them, discerning of their personal joys and sorrows, tolerant of their inconsistencies, and able to help them at times of special need. Her opportunities lie in her personal relationship with the child, with the mother, and with all the children as a group. She has, in contrast to the mother, technical knowledge derived from her training, and an attitude of objectivity towards the children under her care.

Apart from the teacher and her relationship with individual children, their mothers, and the children as a group, the nursery-school setting as a whole makes important contributions to the child's psychological development. It provides a physical setting more appropriate to the level of the child's capacities than the home in which the furniture is scaled to the giant size of adults, in which space is compressed by size of modern dwellings, and in which those around the child are inevitably more concerned with the task of keeping the domestic wheels turning than with creating a situation in which the child can develop new capacities through play – a creative activity which is essential for every child's development.

The nursery school also provides the child with the companionship of others of the same age. It is the child's first experience of being one of a group of equals, and so faces him with the need to develop the capacity for harmonious relationships in such a group.

In their early years, children are undertaking simultaneously three psychological tasks. First, they are building a conception of themselves as a 'self' with a relationship to reality as they begin to conceive it. Second, they are developing a capacity for a relationship with a person, the mother. The mother has enabled the child to develop in these two respects to a considerable extent before going to the nursery school and indeed, at first, the entry into the school is a shock to the personal relationship with the mother. The child faces this shock by developing another capacity, namely the capacity for a personal relationship with someone other than the mother. It is because the nursery teacher is the object of this personal relationship apart from the mother that she must recognize that for the child she is not an 'ordinary' person and cannot behave in an 'ordinary' way. She must, for instance, accept the idea that the child can only gradually come to share her without getting upset.

The capacity to share her will grow as the child successfully makes a third type of development, namely that of the capacity for relationships in which several people are involved. How far any one child will have developed in these three respects by the time of nursery-school age will depend very largely on the nature of that child's previous experience with the mother. The three processes of development will continue side by side.

The process of development, as it continues, creates 'normal' problems which manifest themselves frequently at the nursery school in the child's behaviour. Although the occurrence of such problems is normal and frequent, the child needs help in solving them, for failure here may leave its mark on the child's personality throughout life.

Because young children of pre-school age tend to be the victims of their own strong emotions and aggressiveness, the teacher must at times protect the children from themselves and exert the control and guidance necessary in the immediate situation, and, in addition, ensure the proper provision of satisfying activities in play to help the children to guide their own aggressiveness into constructive channels and to acquire effective skills.

Throughout the whole of this period, there is a two-way process between the home and the school, stresses arising in the one *milieu* being manifested as disturbances of behaviour in the other. When the child's behaviour is disturbed at home, the teacher can often help the mother to understand what is happening from her experience of the child's problems at school.

Through her knowledge of the normal phases of growth, she must also be prepared for sudden and dramatic changes in behaviour and learn to tolerate jealous feelings arising from disturbances in the family setting. Breakdowns in cleanliness, difficulties in feeding and sleeping, retardation in speech, faulty motor activity, these and other symptoms may present themselves as normal problems of growth or, in an exaggerated form, as deviations from the normal.

She will also be faced in the child's early period at the school with a bewildering fluctuation between moods of great dependence and independence; also, even towards the end of the nursery-school age, a confusion between right and wrong, between fantasy and fact, between what is personal property and what belongs to others.

The teacher needs enough knowledge to guide her to the appropriate treatment, either within the nursery school or else by referring to a specialist.

Upon the organization and provision of occupations and activities in the nursery school depends the full flowering of the emotional, social, intellectual, and physical potentialities of the child. The teacher plays an essential role in these activities in combining a sensitivity to and knowledge of children's symbolic language and expression, and an appreciation of the special needs of children within a group. Furthermore, ingenuity and resourcefulness in providing the necessary equipment must be combined with understanding of the value in different forms of play, e.g. dramatic, creative, free, organized, constructional, etc.

In the pre-school years play is the child's principal means of solving the emotional problems that belong to development. Play is also one of the child's methods of expression – a way of telling and asking. The teacher needs a realization of this if she is to help the child with the painful problems which inevitably exist, of which adults are often so unaware, and she needs training which will help her to develop and use this realization of the significance of play to the pre-school child.

Education in the nursery school demands that the teacher shall be ready to exert restraints and controls over such impulses and instinctual desires, common to all children, as are unacceptable in their own communities, at the same time providing the tools and opportunities for the full creative and intellectual development of young children, and the means of expression for their fantasy and dramatic life.

And, finally, inseparable from her work with children, is the teacher's capacity to work in harmony with other members of the staff and to preserve in herself her womanly qualities.

Chapter 29

On Influencing and Being Influenced

No doubt the great stumbling-block in scientific inquiry into human affairs has been the difficulty man has found in recognizing the existence and importance of feelings that are unconscious. Of course people have long shown that they knew of the unconscious; they knew what it was like, for instance, to feel an idea come and go, to recover a lost memory, or to be able to call on inspiration, whether benign or malign. But there is a very great difference between such intuitive flashes of recognition of fact, and the intellectual appreciation of the unconscious and its place in the scheme of things. Great courage was needed for this discovery of unconscious feelings, a discovery which will always be linked with the name of Freud.

Courage was needed, because, once we accept the unconscious, we are on a path which sooner or later takes us to something very painful – the recognition that however much we try to see evil, beastliness, and bad influence as something outside ourselves, or impinging on us from without, in the end we find that whatever things people do and whatever influences actuate them, these are in human nature itself, in fact, in *ourselves*. There certainly can be such a thing as a harmful environment, but (provided we have made a good start) the difficulties we find in coping with such an environment come chiefly from the fact of the existence of essential conflicts within. This, again, man has long known in intuitive flashes; one might say ever since the first human being committed suicide.

Nor does man find it easy to accept as coming from his own nature the good influences and the things he attributes to God.

Our power to think things out about human nature, then, is liable to be blocked by our fear of the full implication of what we find.

Against a background of recognition of the unconscious as well as of the conscious in human nature, one can study details of human relationships with profit. One aspect of this huge subject is indicated by the words: Influencing and Being Influenced.

A study of the place of influence in human relationship has always been of great importance to the teacher, and it has a special interest for the student of social life and of modern politics. This study involves us in a consideration of feelings which are more or less unconscious.

There is one kind of human relationship an understanding of which will help in the elucidation of some of the problems of influence. This kind of human relationship has roots in the early days of the individual's life, when one of the chief contacts with another human being was at feeding-time. Parallel with the ordinary physiological feeding there is a taking in, digesting, retaining, and rejecting, of the things and people and events in the child's environment. Although the child grows up and becomes able to develop other kinds of relationship, this early one persists throughout life to a greater or lesser degree, and in our language we find many a word or phrase which can be used to describe a relationship to food, or equally well to people and inedible things. With this in mind we can look at the problem we are studying, and perhaps see a little further or a little more clearly.

Obviously there can be unsatisfied babies, and also there can be mothers urgently wishing, and wishing in vain, to have their food accepted, and it is possible to describe people who are similarly unsatisfied, or who feel frustrated in their relations to other people.

For instance, there is the person who feels empty and who fears to feel empty, and who fears the extra aggressive quality which emptiness puts into his appetite. This person may, perhaps, be empty for a known reason: a good friend has died, or something valuable has been lost; or through some more subjective cause he is depressed. Such a person has a need to find a new object with which to be filled, a new person who can take the place of the one lost, or a new set of ideas or a new philosophy to replace lost ideals. It can be seen that such a person is particularly liable to be influenced. Unless he can bear with this depression or sadness or hopelessness, and wait for a spontaneous recovery, he must go and seek a new influence, or succumb to whatever powerful influence happens to turn up.

It is also easy to picture a person with a great need to give, to fill people up, to get under their skin, really to prove to himself or herself that what he or she has to give is good. There is unconscious doubt, of course, about this very thing. Such a person must be teaching, organizing, effecting propaganda, getting his or her own way through influencing others to act. As a mother, such a person is liable to overfeed or otherwise to direct her children, and there is a relation between this anxious eagerness to fill and the anxious hunger I have described. There is a fear of anxious hunger in others.

No doubt the normal drive to teach is along these very lines. All of us to some extent need our work for our own mental health, the teacher no less than the doctor or nurse. The normality or abnormality in our drive is largely a matter of degree of anxiety. But, on the whole, I think pupils prefer to feel that teachers do not have this urgent need to teach, this need to teach to keep at arm's length their own personal difficulties.

Now, it can easily be imagined what happens when these extremes meet, and the frustrated giver meets the frustrated receiver. Here is one person empty and anxiously seeking a new influence, and here is another aching to get inside someone and exert influence. In the extreme case, where one person, so to speak, swallows the other whole, the result can be a rather ludicrous impersonation. Such incorporation of one person by another can account for that spurious maturity that we often meet with, or may explain how it is that a person can seem all the time to be acting. A child who is impersonating some hero or heroine may be good, but the goodness somehow seems to be unstable. Another child acts in a bad way, impersonating an admired and feared villain, and you feel the badness is not inherent, it seems compulsive, the child is acting a part. It is a common experience to find a child with an illness which is an imitation of the illness of someone who has just died, and who was dearly loved.

It will be seen that this intimate relationship between the one influencing and the other influenced is a kind of love relationship, and can easily be mistaken for the true article, especially by the persons themselves.

Between the extremes are the majority of teacher–pupil relationships. In these the teacher likes to teach, and gets reassurance out of success, but does not absolutely need success for his or her mental health: also the pupil can enjoy going for what the teacher has to offer, without being compelled by anxiety to act like the teacher, to retain everything as it was taught, or to believe everything any one teacher teaches. The teacher has to be able to tolerate being doubted or suspected, as a mother tolerates her children's varying individual food fads, and the pupil has to be able to tolerate not immediately or reliably getting what feels acceptable.

From this it follows that some of the most eager members of the teaching profession might be limited in their practical work with their pupils exactly because of their keenness, for this keenness can make them unable to tolerate the children's sifting and testing of what is offered them, or their initial reaction of rejection. In practice these are inevitable irksome things, and they cannot be avoided except by unhealthy overriding.

These same considerations apply to the way parents bring up their children; indeed the earlier it comes in a child's life, the more serious must be the effect of the influencing and being influenced type of relationship, when it is put forward as a substitute for love.

If a woman expects to be a mother without ever meeting the child's urge to make a mess at the moment of acute desire to defecate, if she hopes never to have to cope with the problems arising out of the clash between her convenience and the child's spontaneity, we should think her to be shallow in her love. She might override her child's desires, but the result, if successful, would be considered dull; and success of this kind easily turns to failure, since the child's unconscious protest may unexpectedly appear in the form of intractable incontinence. Is it not similar with teaching?

Good teaching demands of the teacher a toleration of the frustrations to his or her spontaneity in giving, or feeding – frustrations that may be felt acutely. The child, in learning to be civilized, naturally also feels frustrations acutely, and is helped in becoming civilized not so much by the teacher's precepts as by the teacher's own ability to bear the frustrations inherent in teaching.

The teacher's frustration does not end with the recognition that teaching is always imperfect, that mistakes are inevitably made, and that sometimes any teacher may act meanly or unfairly, or may actually do bad things. Worse to bear than all this, the teacher's best teaching will be sometimes rejected. Children will bring to the school situation doubts and suspicions that belong to their own characters and experiences, that are part and parcel of their own emotional developmental distortions; also children will always be liable to distort what they find at school, because they will be expecting to find their home environment either reproduced there or else represented by its opposite.

The teacher has to bear with these disappointments, and, in turn, the child has to bear with the moods and character difficulties and inhibitions of the teacher. Some mornings even teachers get out of bed on the wrong side.

The more we look, the more we see that if teachers and pupils are living healthily they are engaged in a mutual sacrifice of spontaneity and independence, and that is almost as important a part of education as the teaching and learning in the set subjects. At any rate, education is poor stuff, even when the subjects are well taught, if this object lesson – 'give and take' – is absent, or is overridden by dominance of one personality over another.

What conclusion can be drawn from all this?

Our thinking out has led us, as thinking about education often does, to the conclusion that nothing is more misleading in the assessment of educational methods than simple academic success or failure. Success may so easily mean no more than that a child has found that the easiest way to deal with a particular teacher, or a particular subject, or with education as a whole, is by subservience, a holding open of the mouth with the eyes shut, or a swallowing whole without critical inspection. This is false, because it means that there is a complete denial of very real doubts and suspicions. Such a state of affairs is unsatisfactory in respect of individual development, but it is meat and drink to a dictator.

In our consideration of influence and its proper place in education, we have come to see that the prostitution of education lies in the misuse of what could almost be called the child's most sacred attribute: *doubts about self*. The dictator knows all about this, and wields power through offering a life free from doubt. How dull!

Chapter 30

Educational Diagnosis

What is there that a doctor can usefully say to a teacher?
Obviously he cannot teach him how to teach, and no one wants
a teacher to take up a therapeutic attitude towards pupils.
Pupils are not patients. At least, they are not patients in relation to the teacher while they are being taught.

When a doctor surveys the field of education, he soon finds
himself asking a question: the whole of a doctor's work is
based on diagnosis; what in teaching corresponds to this in
medical practice?

Diagnosis is so important to a doctor that there was once a
tendency in medical schools to ignore the subject of therapy, or
to relegate it to a corner where it can easily be forgotten. At
the height of this phase of medical education, which was
reached perhaps three or four decades ago, people spoke with
enthusiasm about a new phase in medical education in which
therapy would be the main thing taught. We are now presented with remarkable methods of therapy: penicillin, safe
surgery, immunization against diphtheria, and so on, and the
public is deluded into thinking that the practice of medicine is
thereby improved, little knowing that these very improve-
ments threaten the foundation of good medicine, which is
accurate diagnosis. If an individual is ill and feverish, and is
given an anti-biotic, and gets well, he thinks he is well served,
but sociologically the case is a tragedy, because the doctor is
relieved of the necessity of making a diagnosis by the fact of
the patient's response to the drug, blindly administered. Diagnosis on a scientific basis is the most precious part of our
medical heritage, and distinguishes the medical profession
from the faith healers, and the osteopaths, and all the other
people we consult when we want a quick cure.

The question is, what do we see when we look at the teaching profession that corresponds with this business of diagnosis? It is quite possible that I am wrong, but I feel bound to

say that I can see but little in teaching that is truly equivalent to the deliberate diagnosis of doctors. In my dealings with the teaching profession I am frequently disturbed in mind by the way in which the general mass of children are educated without first being diagnosed. Obvious exceptions spring to the mind, but I think the general statement is true. At any rate, it may be useful for a doctor to show what in his opinion could be gained from something equivalent to diagnosis, if it were seriously undertaken in the teaching world.

First of all, what is already being done in this direction? There is one way in which diagnosis comes in in every school; if a child is objectionable the tendency is for that child to be got rid of, either expelled, or removed by indirect pressure. This may be good for the school, but bad for the child, and most teachers would agree that the best thing is for such children to be eliminated at the beginning, when the Committee or the Headmaster or Headmistress 'finds it unfortunately impossible to take another child at the moment'. However, it is extremely difficult for a Head to be certain that in refusing to admit doubtful cases he at the same time is not keeping out specially interesting children. If there were a scientific method available for selection of pupils, it would doubtless be used.

Scientific method is at hand for measuring available intelligence, the Intelligence Quotient (I.Q.). The various tests are well known and are employed on an increasing scale, though sometimes they are used as if they meant more than they can ever do. An I.Q. can be valuable at both ends of the scale. It is helpful to know by these carefully prepared tests that a child who is not doing well is able to reach an average attainment, thus showing that it is his emotional difficulties that are holding him up, if not actually a fault in the method of teaching; and it is also helpful to know that a child is so far below the average intellectually that he almost certainly has a poor brain which cannot benefit from education designed for children with good brains. In the case of mental defectives the diagnosis is usually fairly obvious before the test is made. There is general recognition that the provision of special schools for the backward, and of occupation centres for the very backward, is an essential part of any education scheme.

So far so good. Diagnosis is being made in so far as scientific method is available. However, most teachers feel that it is natural for their classes to contain both clever and less clever children, and they naturally adapt themselves to the varying needs of their pupils in so far as the classes are not too big for them to be able to do individual work. What troubles teachers is not so much the varying *intellectual* capacity of their children, as their varying *emotional* needs. Even with regard to teaching, some children thrive on having things rammed down their throats, whereas others only learn at their own pace, and in their own way, almost in secret. With regard to discipline, groups vary greatly, and no hard and fast rule works. If kindness works in one school, it fails in another: freedom, kindness, and tolerance can produce casualties, just as an atmosphere of strictness can. And then there is the question of the emotional needs of various sorts of children – the amount of reliance on the personality of the teacher, and the mature and primitive feelings that develop in the children towards the person of the teacher. All these things vary, and although the ordinary good teacher manages to sort them out, there is often a feeling that a few children have to be denied what they obviously need for the sake of the many others, who would be disturbed if the school were to be adapted to the special needs of one or two. These are very big problems that are occupying the minds of teachers day in, day out, and a doctor's suggestion is that more could be done than is being done at present along the lines of diagnosis. Perhaps the trouble is that classification is not yet properly worked out. The following suggestions might help.

In any group of children there are those whose homes are satisfactory and those whose homes are unsatisfactory. The former naturally use their homes for their emotional development. In their case the most important testing out and acting out is done at home, the parents of such children being able and willing to take responsibility. The children come to school for something to be added to their lives; they want to learn lessons. Even if learning is irksome, they want so many hours a day of hard work which will enable them to get through examinations, which can lead to their eventually working in a job like their parents. They expect organization of games, because this cannot be done at home, but playing in the ordinary sense of the word is something which belongs to home, and the fringe of home life. By contrast, the other children come to school for another purpose. They come with the idea that school might possibly provide what their home has failed to provide. They do not come to school to learn, but to find a home from home. This means that they seek a stable emotional situation in which they can exercise their own emotional lability, a group of which they can gradually become a part, a group that can be tested out as to its ability to withstand aggression and to tolerate aggressive ideas. How strange that these two kinds of children find themselves in the same classroom! It should surely be possible to have different types of schools, not by chance, but by planning, adapted to these extreme diagnostic groupings.

Teachers find themselves by temperament more suitable for one or other type of management. The first group of children cries out for teaching proper, with the emphasis on scholastic instruction, and it is with children living in their own satisfactory homes (or with good homes to go back to in the case of boarding-school children) that the most satisfactory teaching is done. On the other hand, with the other group of children without satisfactory homes, the need is for organized school life with suitable staffing arrangements, regular meals, supervision of clothing, management of children's moods and of their extremes of compliance and non-cooperation. The emphasis here is on *management*. In this type of work teachers should be chosen for stability of character, or because of their own satisfactory private lives, rather than because of their ability to put across arithmetic. This cannot be done except in small groups; if there are too many children in the care of one teacher, how can each child be known personally, how can provision be made for day to day changes, and how can a teacher sort out such things as maniacal outbursts, unconsciously determined, from the more conscious testing of authority? In extreme cases the step has to be taken of providing these children with an alternative to home life in the shape of a hostel, this alone giving the school a chance to do some actual teaching. In small hostels there is immense gain from the fact that, because of the smallness of the group, each child can be totally managed over a long period of time in a personal way by a small constant staff. The relation of the staff to what remains of each child's home life is in itself a tricky and time-absorbing business, which further proves the need for the avoidance of large groups in the management of these children.

A sorting out along these lines occurs naturally in private school selection, because there are all types of schools, and all types of masters and mistresses, and gradually through agencies and hearsay parents more or less sort out themselves, and the children find themselves in suitable schools. However, where day schools have to be provided by the State, the matter is quite different. The State has to act in a relatively blind way. Children have to be provided with schooling near the neighbourhood in which they live, and it is difficult to see how there can ever be enough schools in each neighbourhood for these extremes to be catered for. The State can grasp the difference between a mental defective and an intelligent child, and can take note of anti-social behaviour, but the application of anything so subtle as a sorting out of the children who have good homes from those who have not is extremely difficult. If the State attempts to sort out good from bad homes some gross errors will be made, and these errors will necessarily interfere with the especially good parents who are unconventional and who do not plan for appearances.

In spite of these difficulties, it seems to be worth while to draw attention to this sort of fact. Extremes sometimes usefully illustrate ideas. It is easy to say that a child who is anti-social and whose home has failed for one reason or another needs special management, and this can help us to see that so-called 'normal' children can already be divided into those whose homes are coping, and for whom education is a welcome addition, and those who expect from their school the essential qualities lacking in their own home.

The subject is even more complex because of the fact that some of the children who could be classified with those who lack a good home actually have a good home of which they are not able to make use, because of their own personal difficulties. Many families of several children have one who is unmanageable at home. It is a justifiable simplification, however, to make a division between those children whose homes can cope with them and those whose homes cannot cope with them, for the sake of illustrating a point. It would be necessary in a further development of this theme to make a further distinction between those children whose homes have failed them after making a good start, and those children who have had no satisfactory consistent personal introduction to the world at all, not even in early infancy. Along with these latter children will be those whose parents could have given these necessary things had not something interrupted the process, such as an operation, a long stay in hospital, a mother having suddenly to leave the child because of illness, and so on.

In a few words I have tried to show that teaching could very well base itself, as good medical practice does, on diagnosis. I have chosen only one kind of classification in order to make my meaning clear. This does not mean that there are not other and perhaps more important ways of sorting children. Sorting according to age and according to sex has certainly been much discussed among teachers. Further sorting could usefully be done according to psychiatric types. How strange to teach withdrawn and preoccupied children along with the extroverted and those whose goods are in the shop window! How strange to give the same teaching to a child in a depressive phase as is given to that child when the phase has given way to a more care-free mood! How strange to have one technique for the harnessing of true excitement and for the management of the ephemeral and unstable contra-depressive swing, or elated mood!

Of course, teachers do intuitively adapt themselves and their methods of teaching to the various and varying conditions that they meet with. In a sense this idea of classification and diagnosis is already even stale. Yet the suggestion is made here that teaching should be officially based on diagnosis, just as good medical practice is, and that intuitive understanding on the part of the specially talented teachers is not good enough for the profession as a whole. This is particularly important in view of the spread of State planning, which tends always to interfere with the talents of individuals, and to produce quantitative increase of accepted theory and practice.

Chapter 31

Shyness and Nervous Disorders in Children

It is the doctor's business to attend, for the moment at least, to the individual needs of one patient – the patient brought to him for consultation. A doctor, therefore, is perhaps not the right person to talk to teachers, since teachers practically never have the opportunity to confine their attentions to one child at a time. Often they must feel a desire to do what would seem excellent for one child, and yet refrain for fear of causing a disturbance in the group as a whole.

This is not to say, however, that the teacher has no interest in a study of the individual children in his care, and what a doctor can say may possibly cause him to see a little more clearly what is happening when, for instance, a child is shy, or phobic. Increased understanding can lead to lessened anxiety and better management, even when little direct advice can be given.

There is one thing a doctor does that might be done more than it is by teachers. The doctor gets from the parents as clear a picture as he can of the child's past life, and of his present state, and he tries to relate the symptoms for which the child is brought to the child's personality, and to his external and internal experiences. The teacher has not always enough time or has not full opportunity for this, but I would suggest that what opportunity does present itself for diagnosis is not always used. Often the teacher may know what a child's parents are like, especially when they are 'impossible', over-fussy, or neglectful; and the position in the family can be learned. But there is so much more.

Even if the internal development be ignored, a great deal can often be attached to such events as the death of a favourite brother or sister, aunt or grandparent, or, of course, to the loss of one of the parents themselves. I may see a child who was managing quite normally until, say, a big brother was run over and killed, but who since that date has been liable to be morose, to have pains in the limbs, to be sleepless, to find schooling irksome, to make friends only with difficulty. I may easily find that no one has troubled to seek out these facts or to string them together, and the parents who have all the facts at their command have had at the same time to deal with their own grief, and so are liable to have been unconscious of the connexion between the change in the child's state and the family's loss.

The consequence of such a lack of history-taking is that the teacher joins with the school doctor in a set of mistakes in management that can only confuse the child, who longs for someone to bring understanding.

Of course, the aetiology of most of the children's nervousness and shyness is not as simple as this; more often than not there is no clear precipitating external factor, but the teacher's method should be such that, if such a factor exists, it cannot be missed.

I always remember a very simple case of this kind – that of an intelligent girl of twelve who had become nervous at school and enuretic at night. No one seemed to have realized that she was struggling with her grief at her favourite brother's death. This little brother had gone away supposedly for a week or two with an infectious fever, but he had not come home immediately as he developed a pain that turned out to be due to a tuberculous hip. The sister had been glad with the rest of the family that he was placed in a good tuberculosis hospital. In the course of time he suffered much more pain, and when at last he died of generalized tuberculosis, she had been glad again. It was a happy release, they had all said.

Events had taken place in such a way that she never experienced acute grief, and yet grief was there, waiting for acknowledgement. I caught her with an unexpected 'You were very fond of him, weren't you?' which produced loss of control, and floods of tears. The result of this was a return to normal at school, and a cessation of the enuresis at night.

Such an opportunity for direct therapy does not turn up every day, but the case illustrates the helplessness of the teacher and doctor who do not know how to take an accurate history.

Sometimes diagnosis becomes clear only after a good deal of investigation. A girl of ten years was in a school where a good deal of trouble was taken over individuals. I saw her teacher, who said, 'This child is nervous and shy, just like so many others. I was painfully shy myself as a child, and I understand nervousness. In my class I find I can usually manage the nervous children, so that within a few weeks they lose a good deal of their shyness. But this child beats me: she seems quite unchanged by anything I can do; she gets neither better nor worse.'

It happened that this child was treated by psychoanalysis, and the shyness did not leave her until a hidden suspicion had been unveiled and analysed: a severe psychotic illness which could not have cleared up except through analysis. The teacher was right in pointing out the difference between this shy child and others who superficially resembled her. All kindness was a trap for this child, and all gifts were poisoned apples. She could neither learn nor feel secure while she was ill, and she was driven by fear, too, to appear like the other children as far as she was able, so as not to give herself away as needing the help which she had no hope of receiving or accepting. After this child had been treated for a year or so, the same teacher became able to manage her just as she was able to manage the others, and eventually a girl emerged who was a credit to the school.

Many of the children who are excessively nervy have in their psychological make-up an expectation of persecution, and it is helpful to be able to distinguish these from other children. Such children often get persecuted; they practically ask to be bullied – one could almost say that at times they produce bullies among their companions. They do not easily make friends, though they may achieve certain alliances against a common foe.

These children are brought to us with various pains and appetite disorders, but what is interesting is that they often complain that their teacher has hit them.

Fortunately we know that the object of this complaint is not the statement of God's truth. Its object is a much more complex affair, often a delusion pure and simple, sometimes a subtle misstatement, always a signal of distress, a signal of much worse unconscious persecutions, hidden, and so the more terrifying to the child. Of course, there are bad teachers,

213

and there are teachers who hit children spitefully, but it is very seldom that one comes across these by this method. The child's complaint is nearly always a symptom of psychological illness of a persecutory type in the child.

Many children will solve their own delusion-of-persecution problems by continually doing minor wickednesses, thus producing a real persecuting teacher, who constantly punishes. The teacher is forced to strictness by such a child, and one such child in a group may enforce a strict management of the whole group, which is really only 'good' for one child. It may be helpful at times to hand such a child over to some unsuspecting colleague, and so preserve the possibility of sane treatment of the other, saner pupils.

It is, of course, wise to remember that nervousness and shyness have a healthy, normal aspect. In my department I can recognize certain types of psychological disorder by an *absence* of normal shyness. A child will hang round while I am examining another patient, and come straight to me without knowing me, and climb on to my knee. The more normal children are afraid, they make demands of me in the way of technique of reassurance. They even openly prefer their own daddy, and say so.

This normal nervousness is more obviously seen in the case of the toddler. A little child who cannot be made to fear the London streets, or even a thunderstorm, is ill. There are fearful things inside such a child, as there are inside others, but he cannot risk finding them outside, cannot let his imagination run away with him. Parents and teachers who themselves employ the flight to reality as a main defence against the intangible, grotesque, and fantastic, are sometimes deceived into thinking that a child who is not afraid of 'dogs, doctors, and black men' is just sensible and brave. But really the little child should be able to be afraid, to get relief from inside badness by seeing badness in outside persons, things, and situations. Only gradually does reality-testing modify internal fearfulness, and for no one is this process anything like complete. Bluntly, the small child who is not afraid is either pretending, bolstering up his courage, or else he is ill. But if he is ill, and full of fears, he may be reassured, according to his power to see the *goodness* that is in him outside himself, too.

Shyness and nervousness, then, are matters for diagnosis, and for consideration in relation to the age of the child. On the principle that normal children can be taught, and that ill children waste teachers' energy and time, it is important to be able to come to a conclusion as to the normality or abnormality of the symptoms in each individual case; and I have suggested that proper use of history-taking may help in this – that is, if it is combined with a knowledge of the mechanism of the child's emotional development.

Chapter 32

Sex Education in Schools

Children cannot be classed together and described all in a bunch. Their needs vary according to their home influences, the kind of children they are, and their health. However, in a brief statement on this subject of sex education it is convenient to speak generally, and not to try to adapt the main thesis to individual requirements.

Children need three things at the same time:

(1) They need persons around them in whom they can confide simply by virtue of the fact that they are trustworthy human beings with ordinary capacity for human friendship.

(2) They need instruction in biology along with other school subjects – it is assumed that biology means the truth (in so far as it is known) about life, growth, propagation, and the relation of living organisms to environment.

(3) They need continued steady emotional surroundings in which they themselves can discover each in his or her own way the upsurging of sex in the self, and the way in which this alters, enriches, complicates, and initiates human relationships.

Quite another thing is the lecture on sex, given by a person who comes to a school, delivers a talk, and then goes away. It would seem that people with an urge to teach sex to children should be discouraged. Besides, what cannot be done by the school staff cannot be tolerated by the staff either. There is something better than knowledge about sex, and that is the discovery of it by the individual.

In boarding-schools the existence of married staff with growing families in the school surround provides a natural and favourable influence, more stimulating and instructive than many lectures. In day schools the children are able to be in touch with the growing families of relations and neighbours.

The trouble about lectures is that they bring something difficult and intimate into children's lives at moments that are chosen by chance rather than by the accumulation of need in the child.

A further disadvantage of sex talks is that they seldom give a true and complete picture. For instance, the lecturer will have some bias, such as feminism, the idea that the female is passive and the male active, a flight from sex play to mature genital sex, a false theory of mother-love that leaves out the hard features and leaves only sentimentality, and so on.

Even the best sex talks impoverish the subject, which when approached from within, by experiment and experience, has the potential of infinite wealth. But it is only in an atmosphere created by the maturity of the adults that healthy adolescents can discover in themselves the body-and-soul longing for union with body and soul. In spite of these important considerations it seems that there must be room for the real experts who make a special study of sexual function and of the presentation of this sort of knowledge. Would it not be a solution to invite the experts to talk to school staffs and to develop discussions of the subject in an organized way by the teachers? The staff would then be free to act according to their own personal way in their contacts with the children, yet with a firmer foundation of knowledge of facts.

Masturbation is a sexual by-product of great importance in all children. No talk on masturbation can cover the subject, which in any case is so personal and individual that only the private talk with a friend or confidant has value. It is no use telling children in groups that to masturbate is not harmful, because perhaps for one of the group it *is* harmful, compulsive, and a great nuisance, in fact, evidence of psychiatric illness. For the others it may be harmless, and even not any trouble at all, and it is then made complex by being referred to, with the suggestion that it might be harmful. Children do, however, value being able to talk to someone about all these things, and it should have been the mother who was free to discuss absolutely anything that the child can conceive of. If mother could not do this, then others must be available, perhaps even a psychiatric interview needs to be arranged; but the difficulties are not met by sex instruction in class. Moreover, sex instruction scares away the poetry and leaves the function and sex parts high and dry and banal.

It would be more logical to point out in the art class that ideas and imaginative flights have bodily accompaniments, and that these need to be revered, and attended to, as well as ideas.

There is one obvious difficulty for those who have adolescents in their care. It is no use whatever if those who talk about allowing children to discover themselves and each other sexually are blind to the existence of the liability of some of the girls to become pregnant. This problem certainly is a real one, and has to be faced, because the illegitimate child has an unhappy position, and has a much greater task than the ordinary child if he is to make the grade and eventually become a social being; indeed unless adopted at a very early stage, the illegitimate child is unlikely to come through without scars, and perhaps ugly ones. Everyone who manages adolescents must cope with this problem according to his or her own convictions, but public opinion ought to take into account the fact that in the best type of management risks are taken and accidents do occur. In free schools, where there is practically no ban on sex, the illegitimate child is surprisingly rare, and when pregnancies do occur it is usual to find that one at least of the partners is a psychiatric case. There is the child, for instance, who, unconsciously fearing and fleeing from sex play, jumps right over to a spurious sexual maturity. Many children who have had no satisfactory infantile relation to their own mothers reach to inter-personal relationships for the first time in the sexual relationship, which is therefore extremely important to them, although from the onlookers' point of view insecurely mature, because not derived gradually from the immature. If there is a big proportion of such children in a group, sexual supervision must obviously be strict, because society cannot take more than a certain number of illegitimates. On the other hand, in most groups of adolescents the majority are more or less healthy, and in that case the question has to be asked, is their management to be based on what healthy children need or on society's fear of what may happen to a few anti-social or ill members?

Adults hate to think that children ordinarily have a very strong social sense. In the same way adults hate to think that little children have early guilt feelings, and quite regularly parents implant morality where a natural morality could have developed, and would have become a stable and pro-social force.

Ordinary adolescents do not want to produce illegitimate children, and they take steps to see that this does not happen. Given opportunity, they grow in their sex play and sex relationships to the point where they realize that the having of babies is what the whole thing is leading up to. This may take them years. But ordinarily this development comes, and then these new members of human society begin to think in terms of marriage, and of the setting up of the framework in which new babies and children can be.

Sex instruction has very little to do with this natural development which each adolescent must make for himself or herself. A mature and unanxious and unmoralistic environment helps so much that it can almost be said to be necessary. Also the parents and teachers need to be able to stand the surprising antagonism adolescents may develop towards adults, especially towards those who want to help at this critical time of growth.

When the parents are not able to give what is needed, the school staff or the school itself can often do a great deal to make up for this deficiency, but by example and by personal integrity and honesty and devotion and being on the spot to answer questions, and not by organized sex instruction.

For younger children the answer is biology, the objective presentation of nature, with no bowdlerization. At first most little children like to keep and to learn about pets and to collect and understand the ways of flowers and insects. Somewhere in the period before adolescence they can enjoy progressive instruction in the ways of animals, their adaptation to environment, and their ability to adapt environment to themselves. In among all this comes the propagation of the species, and the anatomy and physiology of copulation and pregnancy. The biological instructor that children value will not neglect the dynamic aspects of the relationship between the animal parents and the way family life develops in the evolutionary series. There will not be much need for conscious application of what is taught in this way to human affairs, because it will be so obvious. It is more likely that the children will by subjective elaboration see human feelings and fantasies into the affairs of animals than that they will blindly apply the so-called animal instinctual processes to the affairs of the human race. The teacher of biology, like the teacher of any other subject, will need to be able to direct the pupils towards objectivity and the scientific approach, expecting this discipline to be very painful to some of the children.

The teaching of biology can be one of the most pleasant and even the most exciting of tasks for the teacher, chiefly because so many children value this introduction to the study of what life is about. (Others, of course, come at the meaning of life better through history, or the classics, or in their religious experiences.) But the application of biology to the personal life and feelings of each child is altogether another matter. It is by the delicate answer to the delicate question that the linking up of the general to the particular is done. After all, human beings are not animals; they are animals plus a wealth of fantasy, psyche, soul, or inner world potential or whatever you will. And some children come at the soul through the body and some come to the body through the soul. Active adaptation is the watchword in all child care and education.

To sum up, full and frank information on sex should be available for children, but not as a thing so much as a part of the children's relationship to known and trusted people. Education is no substitute for individual exploration and realization. True inhibitions are resistant to education, and in the average case for which psychotherapy is not available these inhibitions are best dealt with through the understanding of a friend.

Chapter 33

Visiting Children in Hospital*

Every child has a line of life that starts at any rate from birth, and it is our job to see that it does not get broken. There is a continuous process of development within, which can make steady progress only if the care of the infant or small child is steady too. As soon as the infant as a person has begun to make relationships with people, these relationships are very intense and cannot be tampered with without danger. There is no need for me to labour this point since mothers naturally hate to let their children go away until the children are ready for the experience, and of course they are eager to go and see them if they have to be away from home.

At the present time there is a wave of enthusiasm for ward visiting. The trouble with waves of enthusiasm is that they may override real difficulties and sooner or later there comes a reaction. The only sensible thing is to get people to understand the reasons for and against visiting. And there are some really big difficulties from the nursing point of view.

Why, in fact, does a nursing sister do this work? Perhaps at first nursing was just one of many ways of earning a living; but eventually as a nurse she got caught up in the work and became keen on it, and took tremendous trouble to learn all the very complicated techniques; eventually she became a sister. As a sister she works long hours, and this will always be the case because there will never be enough good nursing sisters, and the work is difficult to share out. The nursing

* In the past decade great changes have come about in hospital practice. In many hospitals parents visit freely and they are where necessary admitted with their children. The results are generally recognized as good for the children, good for the parents, and even helpful to the hospital staff in a big proportion of cases. Nevertheless I have kept this chapter as it was written in 1951 because of the fact that the changes have not by any means reached all the hospitals, and also because there are inherent difficulties in the modern method, and these difficulties should be recognized.

sister has absolute responsibility for twenty to thirty children who are not her own. Many of these children are very ill and require skilled handling. And she is responsible for all that is done for them, even for what the junior nurses do when she is not looking. She becomes terribly keen to get the children well, and this may mean following very definite lines laid down by the doctor. In addition to all this she has to be ready to deal with doctors and medical students, and these are human beings too.

When there is no visiting, the Sister takes the child into her care and the very best that is in her is roused. She would much rather be on duty than off duty very often, because she is always wondering what is happening in her ward. Some of the children get very dependent on her and cannot bear her to go off duty without saying good-bye. And they want to know exactly when she is coming back. The whole thing appeals to the best in human nature.

Now what happens when we have visiting? Immediately there is a difference, or at any rate there can be. From now on the responsibility for the child is never wholly with the Sister. This can work wonderfully well, and the Sister may be glad to share responsibility; but if she is very busy, and especially if there are some rather trying cases in the ward, and some rather trying mothers visiting it, it is much simpler to do the whole thing oneself than to share.

You would be surprised if I were to start to tell you things that happen during visiting. After the parents have gone the children are quite often sick, and what they bring up tells tales. Perhaps it does not matter much, this little episode of sickness after visiting, but it may reveal that children have been given ice cream or carrots, and that the child on a diet has had sweets, this completely upsetting the whole investigation on which his future treatment is to be based.

The fact is that in the visiting-hour the Sister has to let go of the control of the situation, and I think she sometimes really has no idea what goes on during that time. And there is no way round this. And, quite apart from food indiscretions, there is the menace of infection.

Another difficulty, as a very good Sister of a ward in a hospital has told me, is that since they have been allowed to visit daily, mothers think that their children are always crying in hospital, which of course is just not true. It is true that if you visit your child, your visits will often cause distress. You keep up the child's memory of you every time you go to the ward. You revive the wish to be home, so it must be that often you will leave the child crying. But this kind of distress, we think, is not nearly as harmful to the child as the distress that has gone over into indifference. If you have to leave the child so long that you are forgotten, the child will recover after a day or two and stop being distressed, and will adopt the nurses and the other children, and will develop a new life. In this case you have been forgotten and you will have to be remembered again afterwards.

It would not be so bad if the mothers were contented to go in and see their children for a few minutes and then go out again; but mothers do not feel like this, naturally. As will be expected, they go into the ward and use the whole time that is allowed. Some seem to be almost 'making love' to their child; they bring presents of all kinds, and especially food, and they demand affectionate response; and then they take quite a long time going, standing waving at the door till the child is absolutely exhausted by the effort of saying good-bye. And the mothers are quite liable to go to the Sister on the way out, and say something about the child's not being warmly enough clad or not having enough to eat for dinner or something like that. Only a few mothers take the moment of leaving as the right opportunity to thank the Sister for what she is doing, which is really quite a big thing. It is very difficult to admit that someone is looking after your own child as well as you could yourself.

So you see that if the Sister were asked, just after the parents have gone: 'Sister, what would you do about visiting if you were a dictator?' she might very likely say, 'I would abolish it.' But still she may agree, at a more favourable moment, that visiting is a natural and a good thing. The doctors and nurses can see it is worth while to allow it if they can stand it, and if the parents can be asked to cooperate.

I was saying that we find that anything that breaks up the child's life into fragments is harmful. Mothers know this, and they welcome daily visiting which makes it possible for them to keep in touch with their children during those unfortunate times when there is a need for hospital care.

It seems to me that when children *feel* ill the whole problem is much easier; everyone understands what to do. Words seem so useless when one is talking to a small child, and they are unnecessary when a child feels very ill. The child just feels that something will be arranged that will help, and if this involves a stay in hospital this is accepted, even if tearfully. But when a child has to be put into hospital at a time when there is no feeling of being unwell, it is altogether different. I remember a child who was playing in the street when suddenly the ambulance came up, and she was whisked away to a fever hospital, although she was feeling well, because the day before it had been discovered at the hospital (through a throat examination) that she was a diphtheria carrier. You can imagine how awful this was for the child, who could not even be allowed to go in and say good-bye to her family. When we cannot explain ourselves we must expect a certain amount of loss of faith; actually, the particular child I am thinking about never really recovered from the experience. Perhaps, if visiting had been allowed, the outcome would have been more happy. If for nothing else it seems to me that the parents should be able to visit such a child so as to be able to take his anger while it is at white heat.

I have spoken of a need for hospital care as being *unfortunate*, but it can work out the other way. When your child is old enough, a hospital experience, or a stay away from home with an aunt, may be very valuable, enabling the home to be looked at from outside. I remember a boy of twelve who said, after he had been away at a convalescent home for a month, 'You know, I don't think I really am my mother's darling. She always gives me everything I want, but she doesn't really love me, somehow.' He was quite right too; his mother was trying hard, but she had big difficulties of her own which got in the way in her dealings with her children, and it was quite healthy for this particular boy to be able to see his mother from a distance. He went back ready to tackle the home situation in a new way.

Because of their own difficulties some parents are not ideal.

How does this affect hospital visiting? Well, if when parents visit they bicker in front of the child it is naturally a very painful thing at the time, and the child worries about it afterwards. Such a thing can seriously affect the child's return to bodily health. And some people just cannot keep promises; they say they will come, or they will bring some special toy or book, but they do not. And then, again, there is the problem of parents who, although they give presents and make clothes and do all sorts of things which of course are very important, just cannot give a hug at the right moment. Such parents may find it easier to love their child in the difficult conditions of a hospital ward. They come early and stay as long as possible, and bring more and more presents. After they have gone the child can hardly breathe. A girl once implored me (it was round about Christmas time), 'Take all those presents off the cot!' She was so weighed down by the burden of the expression of love which had taken this indirect form and had nothing to do with her mood.

It seems to me that the children of overbearing, unreliable, and highly excitable parents can get a great deal of relief for a while from being in hospital *unvisited*. The Sister of the ward has some children like this in her care, and we can see her point of view when she feels at times that *all* children are better unvisited. Also she is looking after the children whose parents live too far away to visit, and, most difficult of all, children who have no parents at all. Naturally, the visiting-hour does not help the Sister in the management of *these* children, who make special demands on her and the nurses because of their poor belief in human beings. For children with no good home a stay in hospital may provide the first good experience. Some of them do not even believe in human beings enough to be sad; they must make friends with anyone who turns up, and when they are alone they rock backwards and forwards, or bang their heads on the pillow, or on the sides of the cot. You have no reason to let your child suffer on account of there being these deprived children in the ward, but at the same time you should know that the Sister's management of these less fortunate children can be made more difficult by the fact that other children are being visited by their own parents.

When all goes well, it may very likely be that the main effect of a stay in hospital is that afterwards the children have a new game; there was 'Fathers and Mothers', and then of course 'Schools', and now it is 'Doctors and Nurses'. Sometimes the victim is the baby, and sometimes it is a doll, a dog, or a cat.

The main thing I want to say is that the introduction of frequent visiting of children in hospital is an important step forward, and is in fact a reform long overdue. I welcome the new tendency as something which lessens distress and which, in the case of children of the toddler age, can easily make all the difference between good and thoroughly bad when a child must spend a certain length of time in hospital. I have drawn attention to the difficulties, which can be very real, because of the fact that I think that hospital visiting is so important.

Nowadays when we go into a children's ward we see a little child standing up in a cot, eager to find someone to talk to, and we may easily be greeted with these words, 'My mummy comes to see me!' This proud boast is a new phenomenon. And I can tell you about a little boy of three who was crying and the nurses were trying hard to find out how to make him happy. Cuddling was no good; he did not want it. At last they found that a certain chair had to be placed beside his cot. This calmed him down but it was some time before he could explain, 'That's for daddy to sit on when he comes to see me tomorrow.'

So you see, there must be something in this visiting business more than just preventing damage; but it is a good idea for parents to try to understand the difficulties so that the doctors and nurses will be able to keep up something which they know is good, but which they also know can spoil the quality of the very responsible work which they are doing for you.

Chapter 34

Aspects of Juvenile Delinquency

Juvenile delinquency is a huge and complex subject, but I will try to say something simple about antisocial children, and the relation of delinquency to deprivation of home life.

You know that in investigation of the several pupils in an approved school diagnosis may range from normal (or healthy) to schizophrenic. However, something binds together all delinquents. What is it?

In an ordinary family, a man and woman, husband and wife, take joint responsibility for their children. Babies are born, mother (supported by father) brings each child along, studying the personality of each, coping with each one's personal problem as it affects society in its smallest unit, the family and the home.

What is the normal child like? Does he just eat and grow and smile sweetly? No, that is not what he is like. A normal child, if he has confidence in father and mother, pulls out all the stops. In the course of time he tries out his power to disrupt, to destroy, to frighten, to wear down, to waste, to wangle, and to appropriate. Everything that takes people to the courts (or to the asylums, for that matter) has its normal equivalent in infancy and early childhood, in the relation of the child to his own home. If the home can stand up to all the child can do to disrupt it, he settles down to play; but business first, the tests must be made, and especially so if there is some doubt as to the stability of the parental set-up and the home (by which I mean so much more than house). At first the child needs to be conscious of a framework if he is to feel free, and if he is to be able to play, to draw his own pictures, to be an irresponsible child.

Why should this be? The fact is that the early stages of emotional development are full of potential conflict and disruption. The relation to external reality is not yet firmly rooted; the personality is not yet well integrated; primitive love has a destructive aim, and the small child has not yet learned to tolerate and cope with instincts. He can come to manage these things, and more, if his surroundings are stable and personal. At the start he absolutely needs to live in a circle of love and strength (with consequent tolerance) if he is not to be too fearful of his own thoughts and of his imaginings to make progress in his emotional development.

Now what happens if the home fails a child before he has got the idea of a framework as part of his own nature? The popular idea is that, finding himself 'free' he proceeds to enjoy himself. This is far from the truth. Finding the framework of his life broken, he no longer feels free. He becomes anxious, and if he has hope he proceeds to look for a framework elsewhere than at home. The child whose home fails to give a feeling of security looks outside his home for the four walls; he still has hope, and he looks to grandparents, uncles and aunts, friends of the family, school. He seeks an external stability without which he may go mad. Provided at the proper time, this stability might have grown into the child like the bones in his body, so that gradually in the course of the first months and years of his life he would have passed on to independence from dependence and a need to be managed. Often a child gets from relations and school what he missed in his own actual home.

The antisocial child is merely looking a little further afield, looking to society instead of to his own family or school to provide the stability he needs if he is to pass through the early and quite essential stages of his emotional growth.

I put it this way. When a child steals sugar he is looking for the good mother, his own, from whom he has a right to take what sweetness is there. In fact this sweetness is his, for he invented her and her sweetness out of his own capacity to love, out of his own primary creativity, whatever that is. He is also looking for his father, one might say, who will protect mother from his attacks on her, attacks made in the exercise of primitive love. When a child steals outside his own home he is still looking for his mother, but he is seeking with more sense of frustration, and increasingly needing to find at the same time the paternal authority that can and will put a limit to the actual effect of his impulsive behaviour, and to the acting out of the ideas that come to him when he is in a state of excitement. In full-blown delinquency it is difficult for us as observers, because what meets us is the child's acute need for the strict father, who will protect mother when she is found. The strict father that the child evokes may also be loving, but he must first be strict and strong. Only when the strict and strong father figure is in evidence can the child regain his primitive love impulses, his sense of guilt, and his wish to mend. Unless he gets into trouble, the delinquent can only become progressively more and more inhibited in love, and consequently more and more depressed and depersonalized, and eventually unable to feel the reality of things at all, except the reality of violence.

Delinquency indicates that some hope remains. You will see that it is not *necessarily* an illness of the child when he behaves antisocially, and antisocial behaviour is at times no more than an S.O.S. for control by strong, loving, confident people. Most delinquents are to some extent ill, however, and the word illness becomes appropriate through the fact that in many cases the sense of security did not come into the child's life early enough to be incorporated into his beliefs. While under strong management an antisocial child may seem to be all right; but give him freedom and he soon feels the threat of madness. So he offends against society (without knowing what he is doing) in order to re-establish control from outside.

The normal child, helped in the initial stages by his own home, grows a capacity to control himself. He develops what is sometimes called an 'internal environment', with a tendency to find good surroundings. The antisocial, ill child, not having had the chance to grow a good 'internal environment', absolutely needs control from without if he is to be happy at all, and if he is to be able to play or work. In between these two extremes of normal and antisocial ill children are children who can still achieve a belief in stability if a continuous experience of control by loving persons can be given them over a period of years. A child of six or seven stands a much better chance of getting help in this way than one of ten or eleven.

In the war many of us had experience of just this belated provision of a stable environment for children deprived of home life, in the hostels for evacuated children, especially for those who were difficult to billet. In the war years children with antisocial tendencies were treated as ill. The specialized schools for maladjusted children which have been replaced by these hostels do prophylactic work for society. They treat delinquency *as an illness* the more easily because most of the children have not yet come before the Juvenile Courts. Here, surely is the place for the treatment of delinquency as an illness of the individual, and here, surely, is the place for research, and opportunity to gain experience. We all know the fine work done in some approved schools, but the fact that most of the children in them have been convicted in a court makes for difficulty.

In these hostels, sometimes called boarding-homes for maladjusted children, there is an opportunity for those who see antisocial behaviour as the S.O.S. of an ill child to play their part, and so to learn. Each hostel or group of hostels under the Ministry of Health in wartime had a committee of management, and in the group with which I was connected the lay committee really interested itself in, and took responsibility for, the details of the hostel work. Surely many magistrates could be elected to such committees, and so get into close contact with the actual management of children who have not yet come before the Juvenile Courts. It is not enough to visit approved schools or hostels, or to hear people talking. The only interesting way is to take some responsibility, even if indirectly, by intelligently supporting those who manage boys and girls who tend towards antisocial behaviour.

In schools for the so-called maladjusted one is free to work with a therapeutic aim, and this makes a lot of difference. Failures will eventually come to the courts, but successes become citizens.

Now to return to the theme of children deprived of home life. Apart from being neglected (in which case they reach the Juvenile Courts as delinquents) they can be dealt with in two ways. They can be given personal psychotherapy, or they can be provided with a strong stable environment with personal care and love, and gradually increasing doses of freedom. As a matter of fact, without this latter the former (personal psychotherapy) is not likely to succeed. And with the provision of a suitable home-substitute, psychotherapy may become unnecessary, which is fortunate because it is practically never available. It will be years before properly-trained psycho-analysts are available even in moderate numbers for giving the personal treatments that are so urgently needed in many cases.

Personal psychotherapy is directed towards enabling the child to complete his or her emotional development. This means many things, including establishing a good capacity for feeling the reality of real things, both external and internal, and establishing the integration of the individual personality. Full emotional development means this and more. After these primitive things, there follow the first feelings of concern and guilt, and the early impulses to make reparation. And in the family itself there are the first triangular situations, and all the complex interpersonal relationships that belong to life at home.

Further, if all this goes well, and if the child becomes able to manage himself and his relationship to grown-ups and to other children, he still has to begin dealing with complications, such as a mother who is depressed, a father with maniacal episodes, a brother with a cruel streak, a sister with fits. The more we think of these things the more we understand why infants and little children absolutely need the background of their own family, and if possible a stability of physical surroundings as well; and from such considerations we see that children deprived of home life must either be provided with something personal and stable when they are yet young enough to make use of it to some extent, or else they must force us later to provide stability in the shape of an approved school, or, in the last resort, four walls in the shape of a prison cell.

In this way I come back to the idea of 'holding', and of meeting dependence. Rather than be compelled to hold an ill child or adult who is antisocial, how much better to 'hold' an infant well at the beginning.

Chapter 35

Roots of Aggression

The reader will have gathered from various odd references scattered throughout this book that I know that babies and children scream and bite and kick and pull their mothers' hair, and have impulses that are aggressive or destructive, or unpleasant one way or another.

The care of babies and children is complicated by destructive episodes that may need management and certainly need understanding. It would help in the understanding of these day to day events if I could make a theoretical statement on the roots of aggression. How can I do justice to this vast and difficult subject, however, while at the same time remembering that many of my readers are not studying psychology but are engaged in child or infant care of a practical kind?

Put in a nutshell, aggression has two meanings. By one meaning it is directly or indirectly a reaction to frustration. By the other meaning it is one of the two main sources of an individual's energy. Immensely complex problems arise out of further consideration of this simple statement, and here I can only begin to elaborate the main theme.

It will be agreed that we cannot just talk about aggressiveness as it shows itself in the life of the child. The subject is wider than that; and in any case we are always dealing with a developing child, and it is the growth of one thing out of another that concerns us most deeply.

Sometimes aggression shows itself plainly, and expends itself, or needs someone to meet it and to do something to prevent damage from being done. Just as often aggressive impulses do not show openly, but they appear in the form of some kind of opposite. It will perhaps be a good idea for me to look at some of the various kinds of opposite of aggression.

But first I must make a general observation. It is wise to assume that fundamentally all individuals are essentially alike, and this in spite of the hereditary factors which make us what we are and make us individually distinct. I mean, there are some features in human nature *that can be found in all infants*, and in all children, and in all people of whatever age, and a comprehensive statement of the development of the human personality from earliest infancy to adult independence would be applicable to all human beings whatever their sex, race, colour of skin, creed, or social setting. Appearances may vary, but there are common denominators in human affairs. One infant may tend to be aggressive and another may seem to show hardly any aggressiveness from the beginning; yet each has the same problem. It is simply that the two children are dealing with their load of aggressive impulses in different ways.

If we look and try to see the start of aggression in an individual what we meet is the fact of infantile movement. This even starts before birth, not only in the twistings of the unborn baby, but also in the more sudden movements of limbs that make the mother say she feels a quickening. A part of the infant moves and by moving meets something. An observer could perhaps call this a hit or a kick, but the substance of hitting or kicking is missing because the infant (unborn or newly born) has not yet become a person who could have a clear reason for an action.

So in every infant there is this tendency to move and to get some kind of muscle pleasure in movement, and to gain from the experience of moving and meeting something. Following this one feature through we could describe the development of an infant by noting a progression from simple movement to actions that express anger, or to states that denote hate and control of hate. We could go on to describe the way that chance hitting may become hurting that is meant to hurt, and along with this we may find a protection of the object that is both loved and hated. Furthermore, we could trace the organization of destructive ideas and impulses in an individual child into a pattern of behaviour; and in healthy development all this can show as the way that conscious and unconscious destructive ideas, and reactions to such ideas, appear in the child's dreaming and playing, and also in aggression that is directed against that which is accepted in the child's immediate environment as worthy of destruction.

We can see that these early infantile hittings lead to a discovery of the world that is not the infant's self, and to the beginnings of a relationship to external objects. What will quite soon be aggressive behaviour is therefore at the start a simple impulse that leads to a movement and to the beginnings of exploration. Aggression is always linked in this way with the establishment of a clear distinction between what is the self and what is not the self.

Having made it clear, I hope, that all human individuals are alike in spite of the fact that each is essentially distinct, I can now refer to some of the many opposites of aggression.

For one example, there is the contrast between the bold and the timid child. In the one the tendency is to obtain the relief that belongs to open expression of aggression and hostility, and in the other there is the tendency to find this aggression not in the self but elsewhere, and to be scared of it, or to be apprehensive in expectation of its coming at the child from the external world. The first child is lucky because he finds out that expressed hostility is limited and expendable, whereas the second child never reaches satisfactory end-points, but goes on expecting trouble. And in some cases trouble really is there.

Some children definitely tend to see their own controlled (repressed) aggressive impulses in the aggression of others. This can develop in an unhealthy way, since the supply of persecution may run short, and have to be made up by delusions. So we find a child always expecting persecution and perhaps becoming aggressive in self-defence against imagined attack. This is an illness, but the pattern can be found as a phase in the development of almost any child.

In looking at another kind of opposite we may contrast the child who is easily aggressive with one that holds the aggression 'inside', and so becomes tense, over-controlled, and serious. There naturally follows a degree of inhibition of all impulses, and so of creativity, for creativity is bound up with the irresponsibility of infancy and childhood and with free-hearted living. Nevertheless, in the case of this latter alternative, although the child loses something in terms of inner freedom it can be said that there is a gain in that self-control has begun to develop, along with some consideration for others, and a protection of the world from what would otherwise be the child's ruthlessness. For in health there develops in each child a capacity to stand in other people's shoes, and to become identified with external objects and persons.

One of the awkward things about excessive self-control is that in a nice child, one who would not hurt a fly, there may come about a periodical break-through of aggressive feelings and behaviour, a temper tantrum, for example, or a vicious action, and this has no positive value for anyone, least of all for the child, who afterwards may not even remember what has happened. All that parents can do here is to find some way of getting through such an awkward episode, and to hope that with the child's growth a more meaningful expression of aggression may evolve.

In another more mature alternative to aggressive behaviour the child dreams. In dreaming, destruction and killing are experienced in fantasy, and this dreaming is associated with any degree of excitement in the body, and is a real experience and not just an intellectual exercise. The child who can manage dreams is becoming ready for all kinds of playing, either alone or with other children. If the dream contains too much destruction or involves too severe a threat to sacred objects, or if chaos supervenes, then the child wakes screaming. Here the mother plays her part by being available and by helping the child to wake from the nightmare so that external reality may play its reassuring part once more. This process of waking may take the child the best part of half an hour. The nightmare itself may be a strangely satisfactory experience for the child.

Here I must make a clear distinction between dreaming and day-dreaming. The stringing together of fantasies during waking life is not what I am referring to. The essential thing about dreaming as opposed to day-dreaming is that the dreamer is asleep, and can be awakened. The dream may be forgotten, but it has been dreamed, and this is significant. (There is also the true dream that spills over into the child's waking life, but that is another story.)

I have spoken of playing, which draws on fantasy and on the total reservoir of what might be dreamed, and of the deeper and even the deepest layers of the unconscious. It will readily be seen what an important part is played in healthy development by the child's acceptance of symbols. One thing 'stands for' another, and the consequence is that there is a great relief from the crude and awkward conflicts that belong to stark truth.

It is awkward when a child loves mother tenderly and also wants to eat her; or when a child loves and hates father at one and the same time, and cannot displace either the hate or the love on to an uncle; or when a child wants to be rid of a new baby and cannot satisfactorily express the feeling by losing a toy. There are some children who are like that and they just suffer.

Ordinarily, however, acceptance of symbols starts early. The acceptance of symbols gives elbow room to the child in his or her living experience. For instance, when infants adopt some special object for cuddling very early on, this stands both for them and for the mother. It is then a symbol of union, like the thumb of a thumb-sucker, and this symbol may itself be attacked, as well as valued beyond all later possessions.

Play, based as it is on the acceptance of symbols, has infinite possibility in it. It enables the child to experience whatever is to be found in his or her personal *inner psychic reality*, which is the basis of the growing sense of identity. There will be aggression there as well as love.

In the maturing individual child there appears another alternative to destruction, and a very important one. This is *construction*. I have tried to describe something of the complex way in which, under favourable environmental conditions, a constructive urge relates to the growing child's personal acceptance of responsibility for the destructive side of his or her nature. It is a most important sign of health in a child when constructive play appears and is maintained. This is something that cannot be implanted, any more than trust can be implanted. It appears in the course of time as a result of the totality of the child's living experiences in the surroundings provided by the parents or those acting as parents.

This relationship between aggression and construction can be tested if we withdraw from a child (or from an adult for that matter) the opportunity to do something for those who are near and dear, or the chance to 'contribute-in', the chance to participate in the satisfaction of family needs. By 'contribute-in' I mean doing things for pleasure, or to be like someone, but at the same time finding that this is what is needed for the happiness of mother, or for the running of the home. It is like 'finding one's niche'. A child participates by pretending to nurse the baby or to make a bed or to use the Hoover or to make pastry, a condition of satisfying participation being that this pretence is taken seriously by someone. If it is laughed at, then it becomes mere mimicry, and the child experiences a sense of physical impotence and uselessness. At this point there may easily be an outbreak in the child of frank aggression or destructiveness.

Apart from experiments, such a state of affairs may come about in the ordinary course of events because no one understands that a child needs to give even more than to receive.

It will be seen that the activity of a healthy infant is characterized by natural movements and a tendency to knock up against things, and that the infant gradually comes to employ these, along with screaming and spitting and the passing of urine and faeces, in the service of anger, hate, revenge. The child comes to love and hate simultaneously, and to accept the contradiction. One of the most important examples of the joining up of aggression and loving comes with the urge to bite, which makes sense from about five months onwards. Eventually this becomes incorporated into the enjoyment that goes with the eating of all kinds of food. Originally, however, it is the good object, the mother's body, that is exciting to bite, and that produces ideas of biting. Thus food comes to be accepted as a symbol of the mother's body, or of the body of the father or any other loved person.

It is all very complicated, and plenty of time is needed for a baby and a child to master aggressive ideas and excitements and to be able to control them without losing the ability to be aggressive at appropriate moments, whether in hating or in loving.

Oscar Wilde said: 'Each man kills the thing he loves.' It is brought to our notice every day that along with loving we must expect hurting. In child care we see that children tend to love the thing they hurt. Hurting is very much a part of child life, and the question is: how will your child find a way of harnessing these aggressive forces to the task of living, loving, playing, and (eventually) working?

*

And this is not all. There is still the question: where is the point of origin of aggression? We have seen that in the development of the newborn infant there are the first natural movements and there is screaming, and that these may be pleasurable but they do not add up to a clearly aggressive meaning because the infant is not yet properly organized as a person. We want to know, however, how it comes about, perhaps quite early, that an infant destroys the world. This is of vital importance because it is the residue of this infantile 'unfused' destruction that may actually destroy the world we live in and love. In infantile magic the world can be annihilated by a closing of the eyes and recreated by a new looking and a new phase of needing. Poisons and explosive weapons give to infantile magic a reality that is the very opposite of magical.

The vast majority of infants receive good enough care in the earliest stages so that some degree of integration is achieved in the personality, and the danger of a massive break-through of entirely senseless destructiveness is rendered unlikely. By way of prevention, the most important thing is for us to recognize the part the parents play in facilitating each infant's maturational processes in the course of family life; and especially we can learn to evaluate the part the mother plays at the very beginning, when the infant's relationship to the mother changes over from a purely physical one to one in which the infant meets the mother's attitude, and when the purely physical is beginning to be enriched and complicated by emotional factors.

But the question remains: do we know about the origin of this force that is inherent in human beings and that underlies destructive activity or its equivalent in suffering under self-control? Behind it all is *magical destruction*. This is normal to infants in the very early stages of their development, and goes side by side with magical creation. Primitive or magical destruction of all objects belongs to the fact that (for the infant) objects change from being part of 'me' to being 'not me', from being subjective phenomena to being perceived objectively. Ordinarily such a change takes place by subtle gradations that follow the gradual changes in the developing infant, but with defective maternal provision these same changes occur suddenly, and in ways that the infant cannot predict.

By taking each infant through this vital stage in early development in a sensitive way the mother gives time for her infant to acquire all sorts of ways of dealing with the shock of recognizing the existence of a world that is outside his or her magical control. If time is allowed for maturational processes, then the infant becomes able to be destructive and becomes able to hate and to kick and to scream instead of magically annihilating that world. In this way *actual aggression is seen to be an achievement*. As compared with magical destruction, aggressive ideas and behaviour take on a positive value, and hate becomes a sign of civilization, when we keep in mind the whole process of the emotional development of the individual, and especially the earliest stages.

In this book I have tried to give an account of just these subtle stages by which, when there is good enough mothering and good enough parentage, the majority of infants do achieve health and a capacity to leave magical control and destruction aside, and to enjoy the aggression that is in them alongside the gratifications, and alongside all the tender relationships and the inner personal riches that go to make up the life of childhood.